MATT

Congratulations
On Graduation
21 MAY 1994

Good Luck

LOUISIANA
PROUD.®

LOUISIANA

PROUD.

A Historical Pictorial of the Real Louisiana
as it began and lives today through
375 original pen and ink illustrations.

Written and Illustrated By
Andy Smith

Edited By
Andrew M. Smith Sr.

Louisiana Proud Press

A Louisiana Proud Press Book
First Edition, 1987
Third Printing, 1990
Fourth Printing, 1992
Published by Louisiana Proud Press
Logo design, cover design, written, illustrated, layout
and design, and production by Andy Smith.
Edited by Andrew M. Smith, Sr.
Quality Crafted in Tallahassee, Florida by Rose Printing Company
Library of Congress Catalogue Card Number 87-80958
International Standard Book Number 0-9618564-0-8
Type set in Clearface at PhotoComp, Baton Rouge, LA
For Information Contact:
Louisiana Proud
6133 Goodwood Blvd.
Baton Rouge, Louisiana 70806

Louisiana Proud

The State of Louisiana has been the subject of many published articles and books. They usually impart a romantic charm as represented by the Plantations and Antebellum homes or by the mystique of the rivers, swamps, and bayous. This edition of the "Louisiana Proud Collection" portrays Louisiana as it was and is. It represents a pictorial history of the growth and development of a unique environment from a vast wilderness to a beautiful monument to the courage and vision of diverse groups of rich and poor people. Some came to pioneer and others came to share in the wealth of the land. All have left their marks in history, by the types of buildings and structures they created to pursue their home and business requirements.

"Louisiana Proud" will help keep the memory of their forefathers and families fresh in the minds of the present and future generations.

Louisiana is unusual in many ways. The semi-tropic temperature, the Mississippi River, the many bayous, the Gulf of Mexico, the vast forests and the rich soil have each contributed to the development of the State. The many foreign countries involved in the discovery and development of the territory left indelible marks, which are unique and very interesting. Louisiana has something to attract the most discerning native and visitor. The revelry of New Orleans, the immensity of the Mississippi, the products of the farms, the richness of its petroleum resources, the grandeur of its antebellum homes, the national historical battlefields and places of history, its ethnic areas and retained customs and its melting pot of industrious, fun-loving people make Louisiana a unique place to visit and live.

Visitors or long time residents of Louisiana will find this book an enjoyable and helpful supplement to the guide books. The art work will show one what to expect in the various cities and towns and the text will provide those interesting details which are always neglected in historical presentations of names, dates, and places. The size and shape of Louisiana makes it possible to tour the entire State in easy stages. A one day trip or a weekend trip will take you to the farthest city no matter from where you start. This book will be at home on your coffee table for quiet study or conversation, or keep it in your car to enliven your passage through the State on special adventures, or just normal travel.

I recommend this book as an introduction and guide for Louisiana residents and visitors who wish to know and understand our most unusual and uniquely picturesque State.

Robert L. Freeman
Lieutenant Governor

SPECIAL THANKS

Special thanks needs to be extended to the three people who were from the start, a big part of this project. Their enthusiasm and input have helped direct its course and on more than one occasion kept the project alive.

The three who were at the beginning are Harry, Kay, and my Father.

Harry Porter sat at fairs; made calls; printed the necessary elements to keep us going and never lost interest.

Kay Ponthieux also put in time at the fairs; made calls all over the state, which resulted in the first poster being produced; traveled miles and miles, climbing in and out of the car to take hundreds of photographs and listened for countless hours about the book.

Andrew M. Smith, Sr. developed all the film; printed thousands of photographs; accompanied me on selling, delivery and photographic trips; made sense out of my writing and encouraged me throughout the entire project.

for
Audrey and Andy Smith,
my parents

From the start, there was no plan.

What you see here is the evolution of events and observations that accumulated over the last five years. The first stages involved photographic trips through the nearby countryside. Barns, rural churches and scenes were the first subjects. Towns and buildings were quick to be incorporated. Each trip was plotted on the map and soon longer and farther trips were made. As the film was developed, certain sites were selected and printed. The first drawings were of these.

As the drawings were developed, they were grouped into a poster format and used as promotional items by banks and chambers of commerce in Louisiana. Seventeen posters were produced.

And all the time the collection was growing.

It was on these trips that a plan started to develop. Photograph every town! Make a photographic record of all the cities in the state; return to the studio and draw. Now the plan was starting to take shape. Five structures in each town were drawn. The collection now consisted of photographs and pen and ink illustrations of almost all the towns in the state.

Louisiana Proud

THE PLAN

The more trips made, the more questions seemed to arise. Why are these towns here? Who were the first settlers? What made them come here to live? What did they do to survive? Another ingredient needed to be added to the collection-People and Events.

This was accomplished by researching over 150 books on the parishes of the state and saving the information about each on computer. The answer to the whys were starting to be revealed along with the events associated with each town. Unsolved mysteries, murders, buried treasure, pirates and indian superstitions were discovered. The naming of the towns, some unique and others misleading, were recorded. The next step was tying the events and histories into a short story.

Now called The Louisiana Proud Collection, it consisted of over 15,000 photographs of the cities, towns and settlements of the state. Over 1200 pen and ink drawings were completed which illustrated over 200 of these towns. More than 200 historical sketches were also written. From the still growing collection, 75 towns, with at least one in every parish, were chosen. They have been grouped in sections and depicted here.

Your are now holding the plan in your hands – or rather the first part. Volumes 2 and 3 will follow the same format until the history of the state, both visually and historically, is complete.

It is hoped that through these words and pictures a part of your history will be revealed to you, and pleasant memories will be invoked. The pride that our forefathers brought to this country is ours. It is what they left behind. It is seen in our customs and traditions, and we are responsible for keeping it intact and passing it on to our young ones.

It's our heritage!
It's our home!

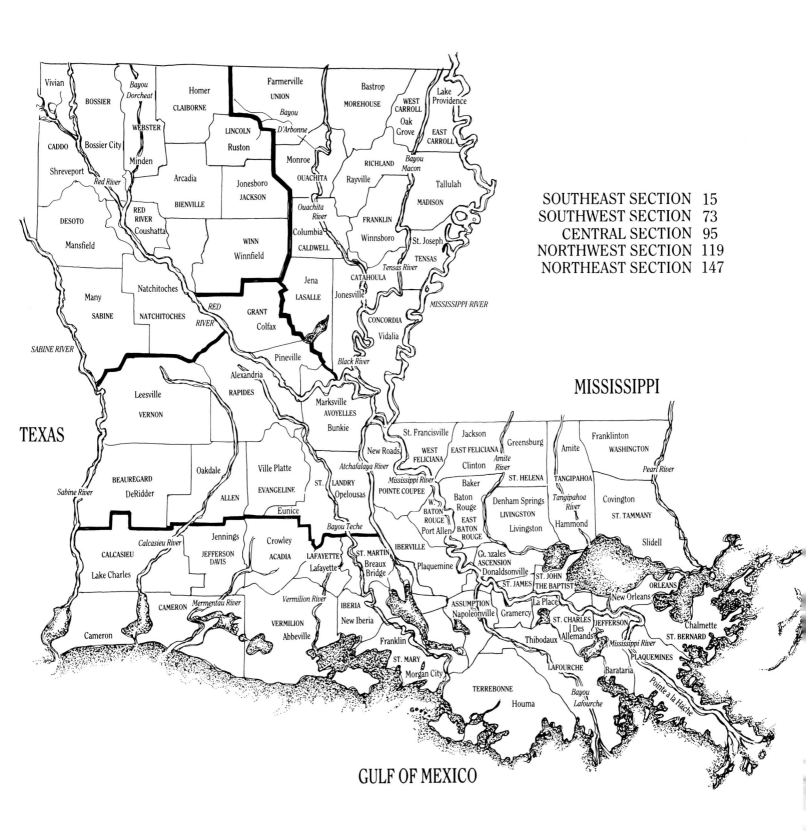

SOUTHEAST SECTION 15
SOUTHWEST SECTION 73
CENTRAL SECTION 95
NORTHWEST SECTION 119
NORTHEAST SECTION 147

TEXAS

MISSISSIPPI

GULF OF MEXICO

Louisiana Proud

CONTENTS

SOUTHEAST SECTION

Amite Tangipahoa Parish	Des Allemands St. Charles Parish
Baker East Baton Rouge Parish	Donaldsonville Ascension Parish
Barataria Jefferson Parish	Franklinton Washington Parish
Chalmette St. Bernard Parish	Gonzales Ascension Parish
Clinton East Feliciana Parish	Gramercy St. James Parish
Covington St. Tammany Parish	Greensburg St. Helena Parish
Denham Springs Livingston Parish	Hammond Tangipahoa Parish

GULF OF MEXICO

Louisiana Proud

Houma
Terrebonne Parish

Jackson
East Feliciana Parish

La Place
St. John the Baptist Parish

Livingston
Livingston Parish

Napoleonville
Assumption Parish

New Orleans
Orleans Parish

New Roads
Pointe Coupee Parish

Plaquemine
Iberville Parish

Pointe a la Hache
Plaquemines Parish

Port Allen
West Baton Rouge Parish

Slidell
St. Tammany Parish

St. Francisville
West Feliciana Parish

Thibodaux
Lafourche Parish

In the middle 1830s, a section of land was claimed by a family of settlers. Six years later a neighbor bought the adjoining section. So it went for almost twenty years as family after family slowly drifted to this area just east of the Choctaw Village. It was a good thing that the last old chief of that village, Baptiste, was friendly, as the early inhabitants could have been driven away easily. Everything was peaceful in this forested area, but it would not remain so.

The team of surveyors hardly had time to stake the railroad line through the area, before three businessmen bought large quantities of land next to the projected depot. A general store was built immediately and soon a thriving business developed with the surrounding area families. The framing of the hotel was just starting when an excursion arrived. Put together by the three, it included a ride by steamer to North Pass and than a rail ride to their new location. Before long a community developed as newcomers and settlers who had been living in the remotest areas were drawn to the tracks.

Was it named for the nearby river? The French had found the Indians very friendly. Could it have been named after the French word friendship (amitie)? Sagamite is the word for a staple corn dish native to the Indians of the area. Is this a possible source? Maybe the French misspelled the Choctaw word Himmita or selected their word "Red Ant" which symbolized thrift among the Choctaw people. Some local tradition recalls this as a place to MEET and others referred to the small community as a-mite of a place.

Amite

Maybe it was one, maybe a combination but the town of Amite grew. Truck, dairy, and strawberry farms rapidly developed as did a thriving lumber industry. Merchants erected stores and soon a town council was holding regular meetings. One citizen who had purchased camels from a traveling circus to work his lands inspired the early ordinance that prohibited pigs, chickens and camels from freely roaming the city streets.

Although it has been housed in five different structures, the courthouse of Tangipahoa has never been located anywhere but in the city of Amite.

Baker

For thirty years, before the coming of the railroad, the area just north of Baton Rouge remained plantation country. In the 1880s a path through the woods was opened, which caused an old settler to remark, "We will all freeze this winter when the north winds come whistling through that hole." The preparation for the railroad had commenced and, when it was completed, this area would witness a new town and a new life.

Built on the plantation of Josephus Baker, the depot was named in his honor. The Post Office was relocated and it, too, took the name of Baker.

Homes, schools, stores and churches concentrated on both sides of the tracks. Sawmills were soon reducing the large timber stands. As the lands were cleared, the fields were converted into cotton fields. The railroad had brought prosperity to the town of Baker.

Eventually the lumber was cut and, when the Boll Weevil entered the area, King Cotton was destroyed and cattle raising took its place. The railroad continued to play a key role in Baker's economy. Now it was transporting people, instead of products, to and from the oil refineries in Baton Rouge.

Louisiana Proud

East Baton Rouge Parish/BAKER 19

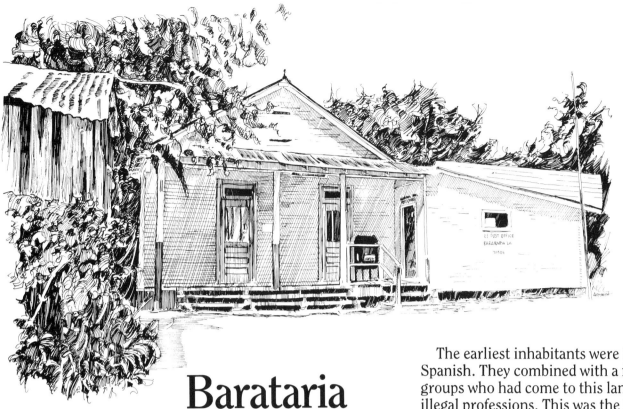

Barataria

Hunters, fisherman, trappers and loggers were the first to settle in these lands called "prairie tremblante." These floating prairies or marshes consisted of a floating morass of tall reeds. Structures were built on elevated sites next to the bayous or on Indian middens or shell banks scattered throughout the marsh. Some built on pilings, driven into the swamp, if it were more convenient to their work. Travel was by pirogue, crafts made from hollowed out cypress trees. The town was built along the course of the water. These elongated cities became known as line settlements. Barataria was one of the first of these settlements.

The earliest inhabitants were French and Spanish. They combined with a few other ethnic groups who had come to this land following illegal professions. This was the land where Jean Lafitte made his headquarters. Pirates and smugglers mingled with the early settlers and, when the pirate trade died out, they remained to take up legitimate livelihoods which the bayous, marshes and swamps provided. It would take the arrival of the steamboat era before any real civilization could be seen in these bayou communities. News, mail and supplies could now be obtained at the small general stores. It was here that the activities of the town centered. They were the trading posts for the hunters, fishermen, trappers and moss gatherers. They acted as community centers where social events were held.

The area grew slowly but the culture has remained intact. Fishing nets drying in the sun, pirogue races, the annual blessing of the fleet, costume balls, candlelight ceremonies in the cemetaries and fais dodo's can still be seen. The giant cypress stands have been almost depleted but the large live oaks, with their moss swaying gently in the breeze, recall the time of the Lafitte pirates and their swashbuckling adventures.

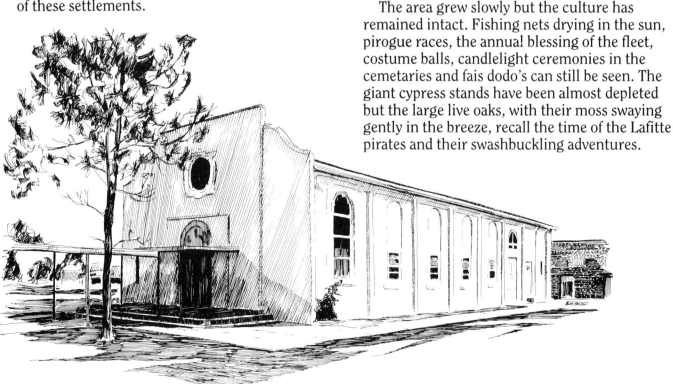

Louisiana Proud

Jefferson Parish/BARATARIA 21

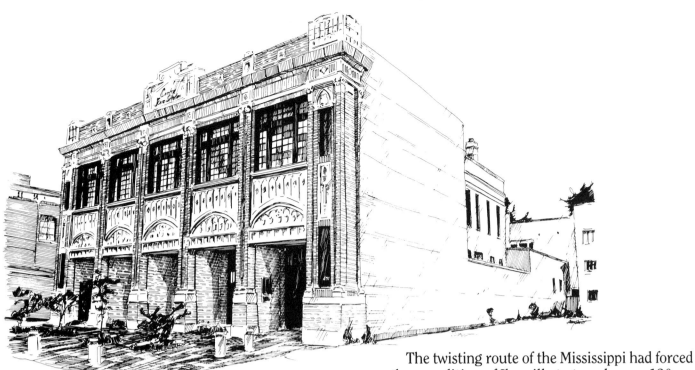

Baton Rouge

The twisting route of the Mississippi had forced the expedition of Iberville to travel some 120 miles since its departure from New Orleans. The slow upriver travel was oftentimes monotonous and the group was delighted when the landscape suddenly started to rise. Delight was replaced by amazement when they came upon the large cypress tree on the top of one of the bluffs. It stood all alone, all its branches had been removed except for a small cluster at the top. The stripped bark revealed the natural red color of its wood. This distinctive landmark marked the hunting grounds of the Bayou Goula and Houma Indians. The French gave it the name Red Stick and built a fort to combat the Indians. It was 1719 and Louisiana was still a part of the West Indies Company. They had granted these lands to Diron d'Artaguette, who tried unsuccessfully to rename the settlement Dironbourg.

Louisiana Proud

Settlement was slow, the population being mostly composed of twenty or so French and Canadian trappers and their Indian wives. It would remain sparsely settled for ten more years, until a group of eighty Acadians arrived in the early 1730s. Even with its population growing, the settlement was kept alive mainly for its strategic location. The large plantation

system that developed needed a place from which to ship their produce to market. In 1812, the first steamboat docked at the settlement named for the giant red stick; it was called the Baton Rouge Landing. The new markets opened up by the steamboats soon had all the surrounding plantations delivering their products here for shipment. A new growth was ignited. Baton Rouge would become the Capital of the State.

Its new prominence would also mean greater disaster during the War Between the States. Occupied during most of the war, the Capitol was burned and the records taken to safer cities. The Reconstruction period was extremely hard on the people, and it was not until the 1880s that the capital officially returned to Baton Rouge.

Chalmette

Two weeks after peace had been declared, the British, after amassing the largest invasion force to ever enter American waters, prepared to capture the City of New Orleans.

Here on the Plains of Chalmette, the British lined up in the early morning mist, prepared to attack. The stillness of the morning hours was suddenly shattered as the drums signaled the attack. The fighting was fierce and when it was over more than two thousand Red Coats lay slaughtered in the fields. They had come up against Andrew Jackson and his army of Creoles, Free Men of Color, Indians, Germans, Acadians and Barataria Pirates led by Jean Lafitte. New Orleans had been saved and the prestige of this new country greatly increased throughout the world.

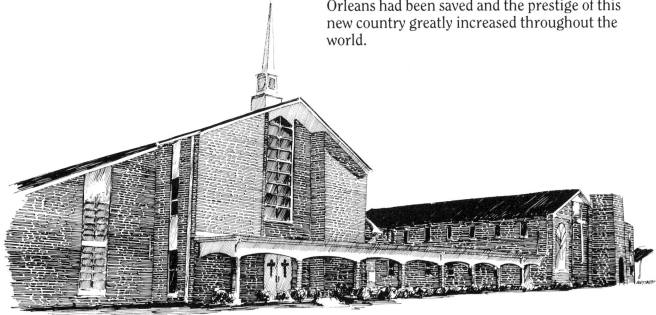

After the war, the people returned to the rich farmlands nurtured by the river and its numerous streams. As the parish was established, this land became part of St. Bernard Parish. The town of Chalmette, where the historic battle was fought, would become the parish seat. With the coming of Industrialism and the proximity of the Mississippi River, the town of Chalmette turned its attention from farming to the shipping and refining of Industrial products.

Louisiana Proud

The quicksands and floods of Thompson's Creek created a barrier to the quick execution of justice in the Feliciana's in the 1820s. When the parish was divided, a new courthouse site had to be established. A survey showed that the exact center of the parish was a barren field, without water or shade. Two and one half miles to the east was a small settlement, located on Pretty Creek, which had plenty of water and trees. It was selected.

In 1825, John Bostwick and George Sebor purchased the lands, laid out the streets and constructed a crude courthouse, jail and hotel. It was named after the governor of New York, Dewitt Clinton, the man responsible for the building of the Erie Canal. At the center of the town was the courthouse square and it was not long before the surrounding blocks were filled with merchants, homes, general stores and saloons.

Clinton

Clinton became the trading post for the rich cotton plantations. The merchants and town prospered. As more and more people flocked to reap the harvest of the land, disputes broke out. To settle questions of boundary, rights of way and debts required the skills of the law profession. Clinton soon was the collecting point for the serious lawyer. Many came to learn their craft and they brought their families with them. It became a population of highly educated people whose first requirements were schools and churches.

Poised around the courthouse square, with its large antebellum structures still standing as a remembrance of its glory days, Clinton retains the flavor and look of days gone by.

Over fifty years had passed since the once-called town of Wharton had become the parish seat. The tone of the times was caught in the incident at Old Landing. The moon was bright as the two river steamers passed. Shouting and waving the passengers acknowledged each other. First a shrill whistle, then a low toot filtered through the darkness. It was then that the horses bolted. Carriages went hurtling through the night as shorebound spectators jumped for safety.

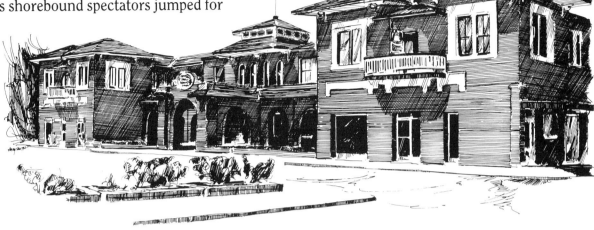

Schooners and horses were the transportation of the times. Wharton, now Covington, was more than the parish seat. It was the shipping point for all the farm produce for miles around, including parts of Georgia and Mississippi. Long lines of produce, including cotton and lumber, were seen clogging the streets on horse drawn wagons while New Orleans bound steamers sat in the Tchefuncte River. Pot holes and lack of bridges made travel very undependable. The floating logs and dead cows in the river, which frequently destroyed the weak bridges that were still standing, did not help the situation.

This area with its virgin forests had long been known for its mineral springs, but when the United States Health Department proclaimed Covington the healthiest spot in the country, the rush began. Hotels sprang up everywhere to accommodate the summer influx of New Orleanians escaping the yellow fever epidemic. Covington entered the days of pleasure and adventure. Balls, parties, hunting, fishing and romantic horseback rides through the unspoiled forest were everyday occurrences.

Covington

Even though Covington was one of the oldest settlements in the state, new business did not develop. Only new hotels were being built and many of them did not survive the numerous fires which started in the late 1890s and continued for several years.

Denham Springs

In the piney woods of Livingson Parish adjacent to the Amite river and at the surface of a low ridge were natural ground water springs. During the early 1800s, Robert Benton ran a ferry across the Amite, while Alexander Hogue was busily clearing land on which to live. The area was at that time referred to as Benton's Ferry.

A few new settlers came to the area but most of the parish was being settled to the south, where the Amite was capable of supporting the larger river boats. At the end of the first quarter of the century, a man from Mississippi arrived. He married the daughter of Alexander, and purchased the original 640 acres of the Hogue tract. He was aware of the mineral springs, but used them only for drinking water for his family and his stock. This man, William Denham, was a farmer. It was the next owner, Stamaty Covas, who developed the springs into a money making adventure. Now called Amite Springs, the settlement advertised and drew people to its hotel and health resort. This short lived enterprise was ended when the War entered the State. The land changed hands again, after the War, as George Minton acquired it for delinquent taxes. He subdivided the tract and sold lots. The post office was called Hill Springs. Confusion resulted because of similar names located in the state and even in the same parish, which resulted in the name being finally changed to Denham Springs.

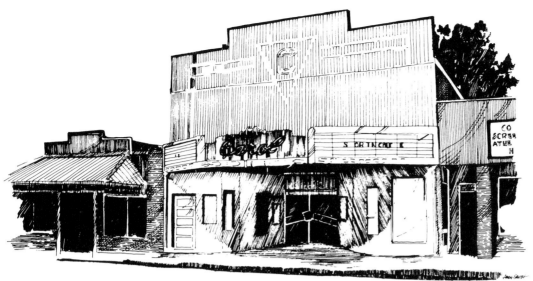

The resort boom and the Denham Springs
Collegiate Institute were the catalyst that brought
the town into the twentieth century. The railroad
established Denham Springs as a shipping point
and made her the hub of a growing truck farming
region. Baton Rouge was not far away and many
residents drove to the oil refineries to work,
while choosing to live in the more peaceful
environment of Denham Springs.

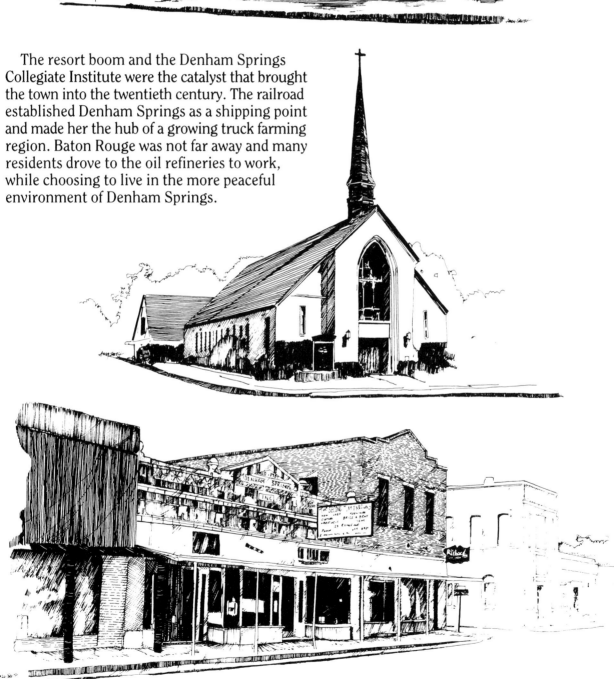

Twenty-one families arrived from Germany at the infant New Orleans in 1719. With their merchandise and belongings, they brought to this new land a fierce determination to live independently. It would be this motivation which would allow a few to survive and pave the way for others of the same nationality to settle. Loading their possessions, they traveled twenty-five miles up the river called "Mitchisipi" and on a small clearing they stopped. Here a mile and one half from the river banks they built "Le premier ancien Village allemand." A second village would be established after floods inundated the first. It did not survive the "great hurricane" of 1721 and finally a third village was established on the higher ground near the river bank. Here they managed to survive until a large number of German immigrants from Arkansas, under the leadership of Chevalier d'Arensbourg, could join them.

This was 1730 and Louisiana was still a wilderness, New Orleans was hardly over ten years old, cotton and sugar cane were yet to be introduced and George Washington was yet to be born. Great oaks, with giant moss draped arms, resisted the puny axes of the new immigrants. The thick underbrush and tangled vines hid the hostile animals and savage Indians. Floods sent them to their roof tops or into the trees as they watched their fields become ruined by the muddy waters. They rebuilt and rebuilt and would not give up. As their crops started producing they could be seen in New Orleans at open markets selling them. They were established by the time the Acadians arrived and their lands were called "the German Coast." Later, sugar plantations would line the coast and fill the passing steamers with their product. The oil industry would replace the old life style and fishing would become more important.

Louisiana Proud

In the village of Des Allemands fishing is of major importance. Catfish are shipped worldwide, and crabmeat and shrimp are processed. Des Allemands is now part of St. Charles Parish. The spirit and industry of the people of St. Charles reflects the influence of the hard working independent nature of the first settlers of the German Coast.

Des Allemands

This was the land of the warlike Chetimaches.

Through the giant virgin forest, taking its water from the Mississippi River, a bayou flowed south. A short distance inland, it divided into two arms. Cradled in these arms were the Indian wigwams, thus the name "The Fork of the Chetimaches."

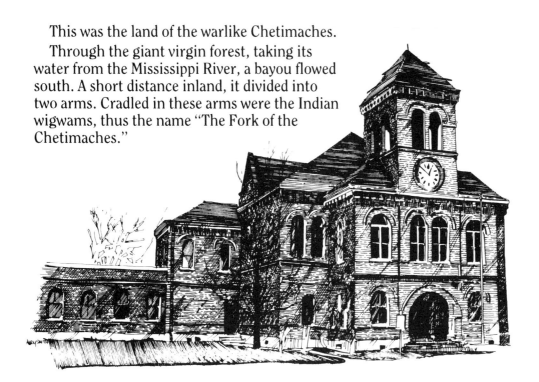

Donaldsonville

Exchanging guns and whiskey for furs, the French called their trading post La Fourche des Chetimaches. Bayou LaFourche, or the Forked Bayou, retains its name today. Some of the exiled Acadians searching for the Land of Evangeline ended their journey in the settlement of La Fourche. The settlement, which had become an important shipping town for Acadian produce and Indian furs, now had a church and was renamed by the Capuchin priest, Ascension.

The early 1800s brought William Donaldson to the area. He purchased land from the Acadian farmers. He laid out streets and the village became a town. It was called La Ville de Donaldson, later Donaldsonville. Twenty-five years later a great honor was bestowed on Donaldsonville. Officially declared the State Capital, it started building the new capitol building, amid protests from New Orleans and Baton Rouge. The legislature voted to return the capital to New Orleans, after the first year, for the primary reason that the New Orleans nightlife had more to offer.

Admiral Farragut warned the people of Donaldsonville against interrupting the Union's river traffic. An old cannon from the Donaldsonville wharf fired upon and killed the pilot of the Yankee steamer Laurel Hill. Farragut stopped the fleet and took action. After the bombardment ended, he sent his soldiers to torch the town.

Around the church, which was spared, the town regrouped and rebuilt. Through Reconstruction, floods and other fires, Donaldsonville remained the parish seat of Ascension.

Andrew Jackson marched through this forested land, among its hills and valleys, and crossed the many small clear streams on his way to New Orleans. It was then part of the large parish of St. Tammany. After Louisiana became a state, the settlers who had built homes found it too far to go to conduct their governmental business. The Parish of Washington was formed and named after the first president. Another statesman's name was used for the town that was to become the new parish seat. It was called Franklinton.

Franklinton

Franklinton had its beginnings on thirty acres of donated land. It was laid out around a parcel designated for a courthouse square. The first inhabitants were farmers and the settlement became a gathering place for their produce which was then shipped to other markets. With the coming of the sawmills, the town started to acquire new settlers, businesses and wealth. Before the War, shipment to other towns, New Orleans and Covington, was by wagon over rugged trails. The herds of cattle were driven across the land to Slidell for rail shipment elsewhere. The 1860s saw railroad tracks being laid closer and closer and, with these new avenues of transporation, Franklinton increased its position as the main shipping and distribution point for this section of the country.

Gonzales

Big Joe Gonzales was the sheriff. He was the law in this wilderness. There were no schools. Land titles were nonexistent, and the post office was ten miles away at New River. The mail for the area of lower New River was received at the store of "To-To" Lamare, still some miles from the settlement.

A horse-powered cotton gin was the first business establishment to be located here. It was capable of producing four bales a day. The packet boat, Katie, ran only on Sundays so you could go to church or visit friends in Donaldsonville. A small general store, operated by the Sheriff's son, soon became a focal point. Through his efforts the village received a post office, which they named Gonzales, in his honor.

The railroad wanted to establish a depot a few miles from there, but the people appealed to the commission and the line was laid in Gonzales. Painted on the Depot was the name Edenborn, the railroad president's name. Again the people complained and it was finally changed to Gonzales to match the post office.

Gonzales has acquired the distinction of being the "City of East Ascension" for the financial, industrial and political influence it has generated in this eastern part of the parish.

Indians owned this land and the River ruled it! Early settlers were often raided by the parties of wandering Indians, or their progress stopped by the mighty flow of water. If they stayed too long they ran the risk of the overflows or yellow fever which were common. It was hard to reach and harder yet to stay.

In 1720, the lands were given to Marquis d'Ancenis. He envisioned a major project of crop cultivation and industry. He chose doctors, skilled workers and even managers. It failed as a fire destroyed his provisions and dreams. Soon the lands became a large Indian village until purchased twenty years later by the Indian Commissioner. Located in the long straight stretch of the river, a plantation developed that became known as Golden Grove. Then in 1850, John McDonough bought the plantation for the Eastern Shore of Maryland Company. Still again in the later part of the 19th century, it was sold to a group of New York business men. Their intent was profit and that meant sugar. The Illinois Central Railroad located a depot here and the area started to develop. Gramercy Park, New York was a highly fashionable residential area. An executive of the New York group lived there and he named this new area after it. It was called Gramercy.

The Gramercy economy became almost solely based on sugar. The land produced it, the mills refined it and the railroads started it on its world wide journey. The area flourished.

Gramercy

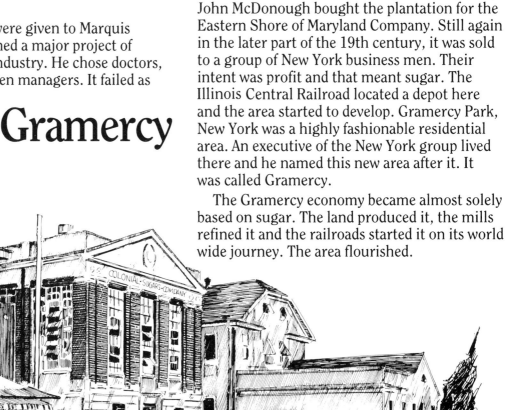

Louisiana Proud

St. James Parish/GRAMERCY 41

Greensburg

The meandering streams, searching their way, left jagged lines in this landscape of gently rolling hills. Here in this dense forest of pine, that seemed to bathe everything with a gentle cast of green, the settlers came.

Along the rivers and streams small stores and mills began to appear. The settlements grew and when the parish was organized the settlement of Greensburg was made the parish seat. The courthouse, school, churches and trade from the surrounding area gave Greensburg the nourishment needed to flourish in this peaceful setting.

As is sometimes the case, appearances are not always as they seem. It was from here that the plans for the overthrow of Spanish rule in West Florida were formulated. It was also from here that armed men marched toward an encounter with the Spanish at the Fort at Baton Rouge.

St. Helena Parish/GREENSBURG 43

Hammond

He came from Sweden and had his pick of the land. Cutting trails as he went, he finally settled in the area that would become the City of Hammond. His name was Peter Hammond and the main street of the town is the trail known as Hammond's Crossing. He started burning tar on his lands which soon grew into a thriving tar and charcoal business.

During the War, Mr. Cate joined him in the area. Bringing with him the technology of shoe manufacturing, he built a sawmill which he used to build his shoe factory. Twice the Yankees destroyed his mill and shoe equipment because he was supplying the Confederate Armies. They left the building standing as a possible future site for a hospital, and Cate was able to re-establish his shoe business after the War.

Settlement continued to be slow for twenty years after the War, until the railroad made its way here. When the Illinois Central started its colonization program, the northern immigrants flocked to the area. The parish, however, continued to grow at a slow pace and a frontier atmosphere prevailed. Men stepped aside for no one and, when their honor was violated, they administered their own justice. Many a man met his death under the shady tree lined streets as the roar of gunfire shattered the peaceful setting. It was not long before the parish acquired the unenviable name "Bloody Tangipahoa."

In the 1830s it was still a virgin forest of moss-covered cypress and other species of trees. Five years earlier a $5 bounty was placed on the heads of all panthers. Repeal came quickly as the coffers were soon empty and repopulation was almost immediate in this dense underbrush. Panthers, bobcats and bears were real dangers to the stranger, as were the snakes and alligators. Raccoons, opossums, and other swamp creatures flourished in abundance. Herds of deer roamed wild. Many varieties of birds earned their daily living fishing in the marsh pools. Among them were hordes of pigeons, whose numbers blocked out the sun and whose combined weight often-times snapped large limbs that were their resting perches. And there was the mosquito. It was this land that soon was to become the site of Houma.

Houma

In 1834, on land donated by Hubert Madison Belanger and Richard Grinage and designated as "standing timber," the permanent settlement was established. Its earliest inhabitants were trappers and some scattered families. Tobias Gibson, a sugar planter, named the town Houma for the Indians of the same tribe, although no Indians had been present in this predominantly French village for some time.

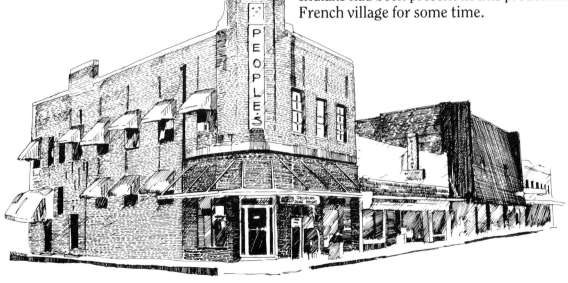

Louisiana Proud

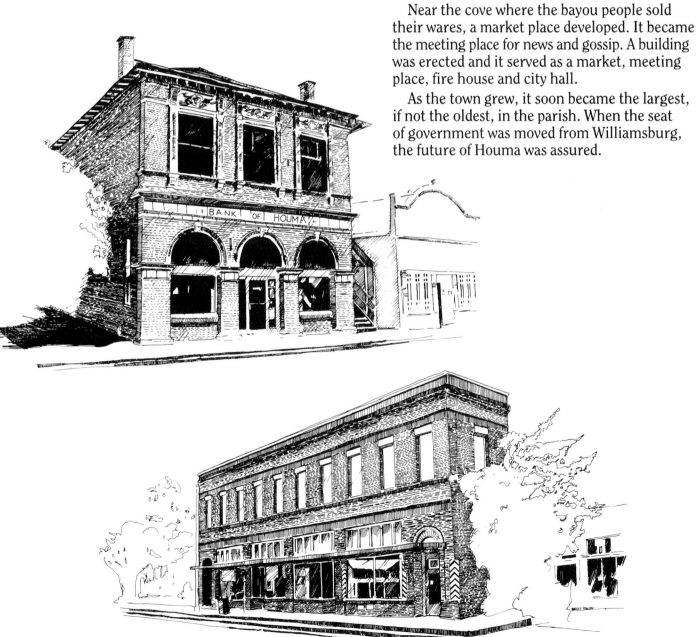

Near the cove where the bayou people sold their wares, a market place developed. It became the meeting place for news and gossip. A building was erected and it served as a market, meeting place, fire house and city hall.

As the town grew, it soon became the largest, if not the oldest, in the parish. When the seat of government was moved from Williamsburg, the future of Houma was assured.

This untamed wilderness on the banks of Thompson's Creek was called Bear Corners by its earliest inhabitants. Later John Horton, on a hunting trip, was so enamored by the setting that he decided to build a town. He laid out the village and called it Buncombe, after his home in North Carolina. Buncombe it remained until the battle of New Orleans. When General Jackson's victorious troops encamped on the banks of the nearby creek, the name was immediately changed to Jackson.

Jackson was designated as the Capital of all of the Felicianas in 1815. Utilizing the inland waterway of Thompson's Creek, Jackson became a thriving bustling town. Many businesses supported by the lumber and cotton industries flourished. Two institutes of higher learning were established with two of their distinguished graduates being Jefferson Davis and Judah P. Benjamin. The location of the seat of government seemed to insure its prominence.

Thompson's Creek had been instrumental in establishing Jackson as the city of commerce, but in 1824 it would also be the reason for the loss of governmental control of the parish. Complaints of inaccessibility by its western inhabitants during times of flooding caused the legislature to divide the parish into East and West. St. Francisville became the capital of the West and the courthouse of the East would be more centrally located in the new town of Clinton.

Jackson survived the separation, and even the War, as it continued to provide services to the interior of the parish. It would take the Boll Weevil and the Great Depression to start its decline.

Jackson

East Feliciana Parish/JACKSON 49

The right angle turn in the Mississippi River resembles the shape of a square bonnet, thus the settlement became known as Bonnet Carre. Here, immigrants fresh from Germany's Thirty Year War were enticed to settle. Boarded on small rotted pest-ridden ships, many never reached their goal. When the first group arrived, the dangers, disease and hardships of the new land discouraged them. Making their way back to New Orleans, they demanded passage back to Germany. Bienville refused and sent them back up river. Soon they were making the land produce and, on many occasions, fed the town of New Orleans when the supply ships did not dock on time.

La Place

Despite the dangerous currents, unpredictable river changes and the spring floods, they learned to live with the river, and soon small shops and homes lined both sides. During the early years of the steamboat, trade crews were paid off here and games of dice and cards, along with the accompanying fights, became legendary. Lafitte also visited the area. Once he sold shipload of West Indian Slaves to the plantation owners here. Known for their fierce independent nature, he knew he could not sell them in New Orleans, but their reputation had not reached this far up river. They soon rebelled and marched with an army of five hundred to New Orleans, intent on murder and looting. All were killed by Hampton's army, and their heads placed on stakes along the river bank to St. John Parish as a warning to others.

French and Acadians moved to the German settlement and marriages were soon taking place. One of the conditions of marriage was that the German men were not alllowed to speak German. Only French was allowed by the brides, and, shortly, the German language was silent.

A Frenchman, Bazile Laplace, came and purchased large tracts of land and, when the railroad established a depot on his property, they gave it the name of the plantation. It was called Laplace. Later the spelling was changed to La Place.

St. John the Baptist Parish/LA PLACE 51

The parish had experienced the explorer Iberville, pirates and slave traders, and had seen its major towns develop along the rivers and streams. Its courthouse had been moved from Van Buren to Springfield, to Port Vincent, and back to Springfield. But it would take almost two hundred years to develop the forested area, which today is the capital of Livingston Parish.

As the forests of other sections in the state were being felled, this remote area remained untouched. The Lyon Lumber Company had established a mill in St. John the Baptist Parish at Garyville. As the lumber was cut, the railroad line was extended farther and farther north. In only twelve years it had reached the Amite River. The cypress had all been cut, the mill adapted to pine, and all that was needed was land and transportation across the river. The Lumber Company acquired large tracts of land near the community of Doyle, and, by using the Baton Rouge to Hammond Railroad facility, were able to cross the river and continue its line. The saw mill was reassembled and a station built, complete with a coal chute and repair buildings. The Company owned the town, employed the people and gave it the name Livingston. Access by the railroad soon placed Livingston as a leader of the parish. When the company had cut the woods and moved out, the town was left with only twelve families. But the railroad remained, and access to Baton Rouge and Hammond encouraged growth as a shipping point distribution center for a large area. In the early 1940s, the courthouse was relocated at Livingston and the town continued to grow as new lumber interest restored stability to the community.

Livingston

Napoleonville City or Napoleonville was named either by a French soldier who fought with Napoleon, or the Napoleon family which played a prominent role in the history of the community. The Napoleon family donated the land for the townsite. The town was also called "Courthouse" ninety years before the present buff colored brick structure, guarded by the square clock tower, was built.

Napoleonville

Exiled Acadians who overcame hundreds of miles of land and river wilderness arrived in this area called "terre gras" or fat land. To this new home they brought the lilied banner of France and its customs. The settlement along the bayou was called Canal or Courthouse. It was not until some fifty years had passed, when the parish was established, that the settlement became known as Napoleonville.

Napoleonville was already a thriving market-place at the beginning of the 19th century and saw the desecration of one of its churches by Federal troops. Stabling their horses in the Christ Episcopal Church, they used the stained glass window for target practice.

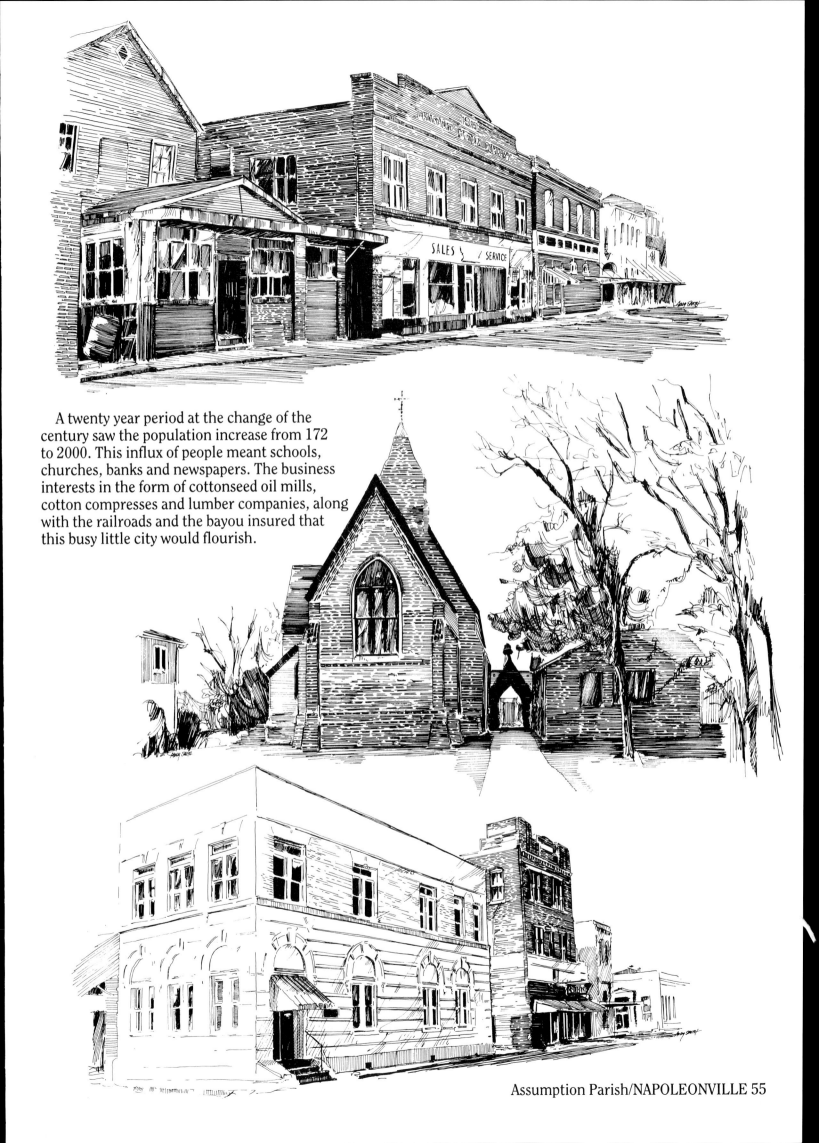

A twenty year period at the change of the century saw the population increase from 172 to 2000. This influx of people meant schools, churches, banks and newspapers. The business interests in the form of cottonseed oil mills, cotton compresses and lumber companies, along with the railroads and the bayou insured that this busy little city would flourish.

New Orleans

Where the river gracefully turns in the shape of a crescent, the town was laid out in the shape of a giant square. It would grow into a wealthy city. A place of riverboats and sailing ships, of balls and banquets, hotels and restaurants and where cotton and sugar were kings. A place where the opera and theater flourished along side the gambling, duelling, bawdy houses and voodoo.

The town which was named by the French, Nouvelle-Orleans, in honor of the regent of France, Louis Phillippe duc d' Orleans, has been called many names. Creole City, the City Care Forgot, Carnival City, Queen City of the South, and the oldest and most descriptive, Crescent City, have all been used in describing the City of New Orleans.

It was 1717, eighteen years after Iberville and his brother Bienville first settled the new territory named Louisiana. Iberville had died the year before and it was Bienville who assumed the task of moving the seat of government of the Louisiana colony from the Biloxi Fort. What the Indians called the Mississippi or "great water", the French renamed the Fleuve Saint Louis. Leading from this mighty river to a large lake was an old Indian portage. It was here that Bienville chose to build. At this site, a town, which had been named four years earlier in France, would be built.

To solve the problem of settlers, the French Government sent eighty convicts to the new lands. Saltmakers, banished for evading the tax, were the first to start clearing the lands. As the dense stands of cypress trees and heavy underbrush were cleared, carpenters and other craftsmen joined them.

Heeding his Indian guide's advice, Iberville stopped his ascent up the river at the small debris-filled stream. Clearing the way as they went, it took nine hours before his men were able to push their flat boats through to the other side. Here he discovered a new body of water, another river. After three days of exploring, he found that it was actually the same river which, by forming a new channel, had created an island. By using this channel he could save twenty-two miles of travel and he named it "The Point of the Cut Off" or Pointe Coupee. Soon a small settlement grew on the northern tip of the cut off, about a year before New Orleans was established.

Basically it was a trading post for the French hunters and trappers who roamed its forests. Then as the planters discovered the rich soil, tobacco and indigo were raised and shipped from here. As the ends of the cut off slowly filled again, the town was lost, as was the river traffic that supplied the area. All that remained was a large clear ox-bow lake that took the name "Fausse Riviere".

A church was built. The community which developed was called St. Mary, after the name of the church. It remained small and served mostly the surrounding plantations. The name was almost changed to Rose Lake, in honor of the wild roses which grew in profusion around the shores of the lake.

New Roads

Around the 1850s, the need to connect the commercial establishments on the river with the plantations on False River resulted in the establishment of the Chemin Neuf. This was an extension of the Bayou Sara Ferry Road. The seat of government was moved to the village of St. Mary. It became known as Chemin Neuf or in English, New Roads.

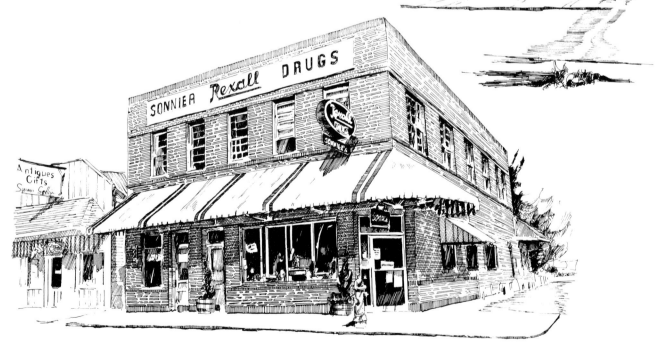

Before America had finished her Revolution, the first settlers had made friends with the Indians along this bayou, and broke bread with them. The Indian mixture of dried persimmon fruit and flour soon became a staple of the trading post people of the area. Growing wild along the banks of an inland bayou, this fruit gave its name to the waterway and settlement that followed. It was called the area of the Plaquemines by the French. Many years passed as the Indians and the French met here and swapped their furs with New Orleans bound merchants.

The bayou, although impassable for long stretches, was the main route for travel inland. Seeing the need for a town to supply and house the many travelers, Thomas Pipkin began to develop the town which later became Plaquemine. He subdivided the land and advertized to all, "Come to the Town of Iberville, gateway to the interior, where bi-weekly steamboats and sawmills await the new and ambitious."

He had somewhat elaborated on the truth.

True, the steamboat did run twice a week, when the bayou was not jammed with fallen logs, and there was a small sawmill in the area. The constant pools of mud deposited on the site during overflows, or breaks in the small levees, and the yearly threat of malaria were left for their discovery by the new arrivals. Still, they came.

When the big sawmill came, the lumber boom was not far behind. Huge sugar plantations surrounded the town, and Plaquemine, as it was now called, became a major lumber and shipping center. Its location on the river and its bountiful supply of commerce assured the stopping of all the major steamboat lines. Pipkin's original town had been reclaimed by the caving banks of the Mississippi by now, but the new town was prospering enough to become the parish seat.

Louisiana Proud

Plaquemine

Before the War, a traveler found himself in a well built bustling town boasting a sound economy and thriving shops. Never again was he left stranded in pools of mud, for now splendid hotels waited to comfort his tired bones. For entertainment and nourishment, the Texas or Magnolia Coffee Houses awaited his pleasures. With the War, the rerouting of the bayou traffic, and the timber supply exhausted, the prosperity started to diminish and the area settled to a slower pace.

LaSalle was the first man, other than the roving bands of Indians, to see these fertile lands. Iberville entered the continent via the same large waterway which would later be called the Mississippi River. The River has played a key role in the development of the parish. Along its banks were erected numerous forts by both the Spanish and French. New Orleans was supplied by passage up the river and, on more than one occasion, the sale of illegal contraband slaves was carried out by Jean Lafitte.

The first inhabitants were left here by the Western Company in the 1720s, and they were soon joined by the Acadians. Along the river and bayous, small settlements developed, while most of the land was turned into plantations.

When the parish was organized, the largest town was made the seat of government. It was located in the curve of the river. On the east bank, at the curve, is a point of land in the shape of an ax or hatchet-thus the name, Pointe a la Hache. Like all the towns of Plaquemines Parish, it remained rather small, and became a distribution point for the produce of the rich lands of the plantations. Hurricanes and floods have had their way with the countryside, but the rugged independent people always endured and rebuilt.

Pointe a la Hache

Port Allen

Michael Mahier, a French doctor in the employ of the Spanish crown, who was stationed at Baton Rouge, acquired the lands directly across the River in the Parish of West Baton Rouge. He laid out a town, complete with streets, lots and a public square. Formerly it was christened "la Ville de St. Michel," but soon became known by the name St. Michel. Business prospered and new settlers gave the town a solid base. Its foundation was not as solid, however, as, in only three short years, the river had claimed half the town. Today all is lost of the original site. The people moved farther back and when the original lands were purchased, the Town of West Baton Rouge was established.

Just across the plantation fields, another settlement was growing. It was called Sunnyside. This settlement soon displaced the Town of West Baton Rouge as the center of financial and cultural events in the parish. The Post Office was established in the 1870s and had to have an official name. Called "the Port," after the completion of the Baton Rouge, Grosse Tete, and Opelousas Railroad, it officially became known as Port Allen in honor of the Civil War governor of Louisiana, Henry Watkins Allen.

At one time Port Allen was as important as Baton Rouge and almost as large, and had regular ferry traffic between the two governmental seats. The River and the War took its toll on the West Bank, as Baton Rouge emerged as the dominant city at this point on the River.

Louisiana Proud

West Baton Rouge Parish/PORT ALLEN 65

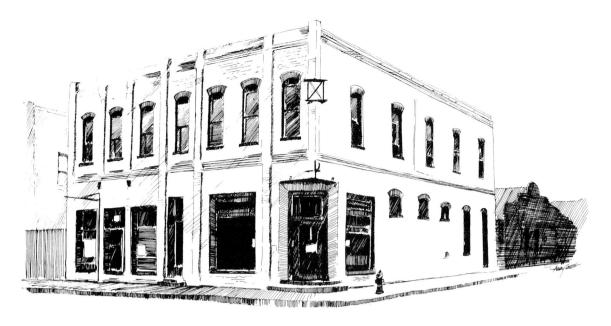

A statesman, a politican, the minister to Mexico and, in the 1850s, he was the political boss of Louisiana. When Louisiana seceded from the Union, he became the Confederate Commissioner to France. Captured, jailed, and finally set free, he died in exile never having seen the town which took his name.

Slidell

The last town to develop in St. Tammany became known as Slidell in honor of the influential John Slidell. In the early 1880s, Slidell was located on the New Orleans Northeastern Railroad tracks. It was an unruly place until the Committee of Safety invited the citizens of questionable character to leave. Soon brickyards with the capacity to turn out enormous production were operating at full capacity. Sawmills and lumber yards were producing. The Slidell area had become the Industrial leader in the Parish and was growing at a boom rate.

When Mississippi voted dry, a large "jug trade" sprang up, and more than one met an early death on these floating saloons. As the population increased and the supporting business establishments grew, the area became quieter. The climate was healthy, water cool and clear, and there were large areas for stock to graze and fertile fields to plow.

The rivalry with Covington about the parish seat became a hot issue when a new courthouse was to be built. Slidell wanted the parish seat moved here because after all their town was the most important town, economically, in the parish. The courthouse remained in Covington and things settled back to the way they were.

St. Francisville

The first white men came to this land, named Nueva Feliciana by Ponce de Leon, and settled among the Indians during the early 1700s. For fifty years the settlement under French rule progressed slowly, guarded by the old ruins of Fort Rosalie and the dead of the local inhabitants. Located on "Sainte Reine", a high ridge that ran along the river, it became a burial ground for the people of the surrounding area including those of Pointe Coupee who were ferried across the river. After Great Britain secured control of the Florida Parishes, settlement increased.

By the time the parish was divided into East and West Feliciana in 1824, its frontier days were over. Population, plantations, and politicans were firmly entrenched. There was to be only one center of commerce in West Feliciana. On the ridge overlooking the river grew the town of St. Francisville, named after St. Francis of Assisi. Located at the foot of the ridge flourished her sister city, Bayou Sara. Together they furnished the large backcountry with access to the world. Cotton and sugar were the principal crops of the large plantations. The wharves of Bayou Sara were full and both towns prospered. The antebellum period was at its height, as steamboats were constantly arriving, merchants were thriving, mansions were being built and stage lines connecting Baton Rouge, Clinton, Jackson and Natchez were established. In the 1830s, the West Feliciana Railroad was established.

By the time the river had washed away Bayou Sara, St. Francisville was firmly established as a center of political and economical importance and would remain so until the 1860s when the War came down the river.

West Feliciana Parish/ST. FRANCISVILLE 69

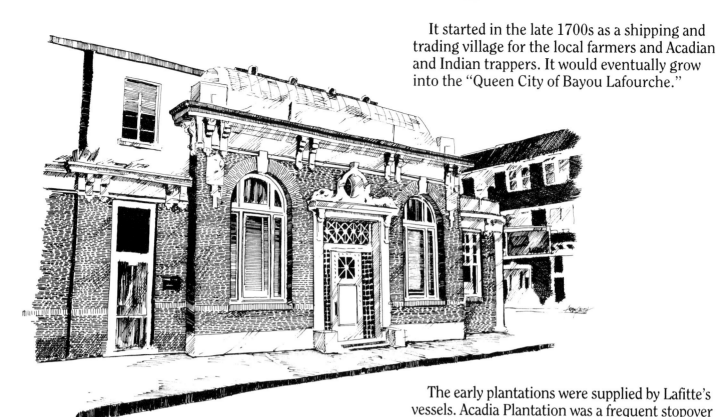

It started in the late 1700s as a shipping and trading village for the local farmers and Acadian and Indian trappers. It would eventually grow into the "Queen City of Bayou Lafourche."

The early plantations were supplied by Lafitte's vessels. Acadia Plantation was a frequent stopover place. It belonged to the Bowie Brothers, who were then engaged with Lafitte in the illegal slave trade. When Henry Thibodaux, planter, legislator and governor of Louisiana, donated land for a courthouse, jail and market in 1820, the trading post settlement became a town. As the parish seat, its future was secure. New families moved in and built their homes in the town known as Thibodauxville.

Thibodauxville became the financial center of the Parish when the bank was established. Trade and politics added to its importance, which prompted Henry Clay during his bid for Presidency, to make Thibodaux a stop for a campaign speech.

Prosperity was common, the steamboats were frequent visitors, so, when the news of the approaching railroad reached Thibodaux, the prominent citizens reacted. In order to prevent the dirt and noise and the cluttering of the town, the tracks were diverted three miles South. As the steamboat traffic diminished, the town came to regret its decision and, even today, no main railroad line passes through the town.

Thibodaux

Louisiana Proud

LaFourche Parish/THIBODAUX 71

SOUTHWEST SECTION

Abbeville
Vermilion Parish

Breaux Bridge
St. Martin Parish

Cameron
Cameron Parish

Crowley
Acadia Parish

Franklin
St. Mary Parish

Jennings
Jefferson Davis Parish

Lafayette
Lafayette Parish

Lake Charles
Calcasieu Parish

Morgan City
St. Mary Parish

New Iberia
Iberia Parish

Sabine River

TEXAS

Calcasieu River

CALCASIEU

Lake Charles

Jennings

JEFFERSON
DAVIS

Crowley

ACADIA

Bayou Teche

LAFAYETTE

Lafayette

ST. MARTIN

Breaux
Bridge

CAMERON

Mermentau River

Vermilion River

IBERIA

New Iberia

Cameron

VERMILION

Abbeville

Franklin

ST. MARY

Morgan City

GULF OF MEXICO

Louisiana Proud

HEYWOOD BUILDING

PHILCO

DAIGLE'S TV CLINIC

He was a priest and he lived in Vermilionville. For years he traveled the twenty miles by horse and pirogue to minister to his people. All he wanted was a small piece of land on which to build a church. Pont-Perry was the village of note in this land of sparsely populated scattered ranches and communities. Its location on the Vermilion river and access to the bridge insured its prominence. The people of Perry's Bridge offered him a small piece of land that was low and swampy. He refused.

Abbeville

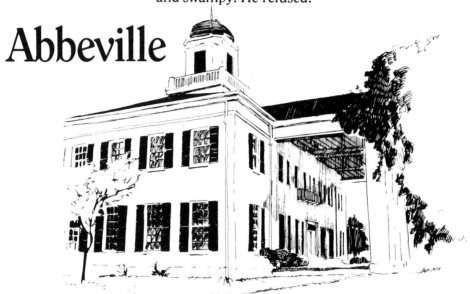

This man of God was Father Megret and, knowing of a large tract of good land about three miles up river, he purchased it for $900. He laid out streets and small farm plots, which were sold under his Church Real Estate Plan. It worked, and soon the little settlement around the church became larger and larger. The Acadian settlers of the area congregated here and called their town La Chappelle. When Megret left Vermilionville to spend all his time at the new chapel, he changed the name to honor his home town of Abbeville, France.

For a while a bitter contest between Abbeville and Perry's Bridge raged over which would be the parish seat. Finally, after switching from year to year, the seat of government was permanently established at Abbeville, and the town that did not want the church soon faded into oblivion. Father Megret had died a few years earlier during a yellow fever epidemic, but his picture still hangs in the courthouse of the town he founded.

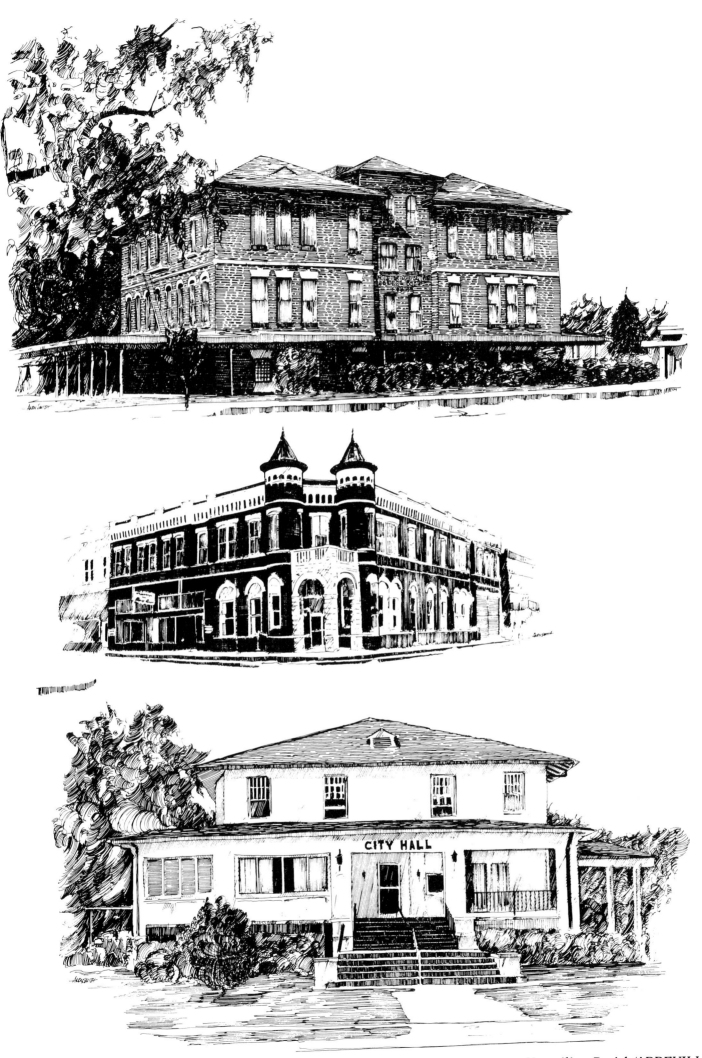

Breaux Bridge

It was called La Pointe in the Spanish Census of 1766 and it designated the bend or point in the Bayou called Teche.

Only Acadians were living in the area by the 1800s, mainly hunting and raising cattle for their livelihood. The earliest settlers claimed the land, and a small trading settlement was built around the bend in the bayou. Its name was changed to that of a property owner, Firmin Breaux. When the river was finally spanned, the settlement became known as Breaux Bridge.

No records exist as to when the first bridge was built, but it, or one that replaced it was seen burning during the War. Forced to flee up the bayou to Opelousas, the Confederates were seen in the town only minutes before the Federals reached them. They were there taking on supplies which had been delivered the day before by the Steamboats Darby, Louise, Blue Hammock and Uncle Tom. Leaving behind only a few snipers to slow the Yankees, they crossed the river and torched the bridge. Others have taken their place, first wooden and later steel. The self pride, and religious convictions which had been instilled in them by their Acadian ancestors kept them alive even through much personal suffering which was inflicted during the War. Their spirit and family unity soon restored their easy, carefree and friendly way of life.

St. Martin Parish/BREAUX BRIDGE 77

Almost 150 years ago, small groups of individuals made their way down the rivers to the edge of the sea. They were attracted by a large waving sea of grass. The small area of uplands attracted the agriculturists, while the great abundance of game brought the hunters and sportsmen. These groups were followed by the settlers who found no farms, no churches, no schools, but only vast stretches of wilderness inhabited by the wild beasts and an occasional band of Indian hunters. As they continued to come, a town began to appear and, with the establishment of the post office, became officially known as Leesburg.

Cameron

A newspaper article in the late 1880s reported about the parish known as Cameron. It told about the parish seat of Leesburg which rested next to the coast. Leesburg contained a courthouse, jail and one or two stores, but no saloons. The District Court met only once and had made no decisions, which probably accounts for no practicing attorneys in the parish. It went on to explain that the rewards of living on the coast were numerous, but also warned of the ever present danger of the storms that brewed offshore.

The name Leesburg became confusing for the post office as Louisiana already had a Leesville and Leeville. To avoid confusion, they changed it to the name of the parish, Cameron.

The explosion in the Opelousas Courthouse set off a chain reaction of events. Washington wanted the new courthouse there. Rayne wanted either the new courthouse or the establishment of a new parish of which they would be the parish seat. The Opelousas politicans, fearing loss of their hold on the government, opted for the latter and the Parish of Acadia was formed.

The battle for the parish seat was on. Rayne and Prairie Hayes were the front runners, each extolling its virtues.

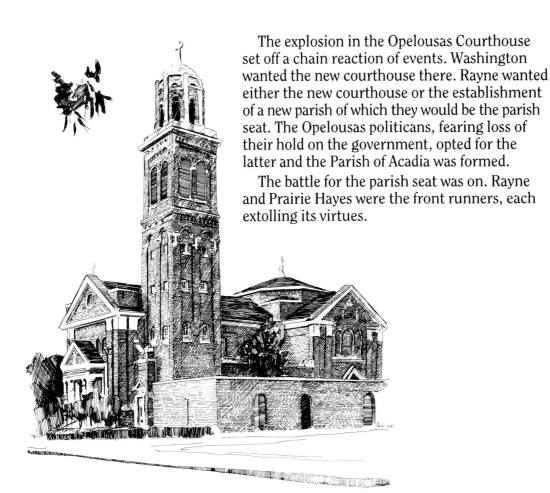

Crowley

No one even considered Houstch. Four months before the new parish was formed, a group of men in this town decided to move it six miles down the Louisiana Western Railroad Line and form a new town. It was to be called Parkerson-ville in honor of the general agent of the railroad. Mr. Parkerson declined, so the honor of having the town named after him fell to Patrick Crowley, who was in charge of the nearby spur-track known as the Crowley Switch.

So sure were they about getting the parish seat, that the two newspapers in Rayne did not report all the activity to the west, which resembled a beehive. A depot was in place in only five hours after being taken from nearby Estherwood by rail. In two weeks the town was gaining state-wide recognition, as, magically, it seemed to appear out of the prairie. Rumors, as if carried on the wind, started being heard of a third contender for the governmental seat. The people of Rayne became upset about this new threat and, when the Opelousas Courier advertised the Big Auction, their fears grew deeper.

The leaders of Crowley had more than an auction, they had a party. Low fares and frequent stops between Lafayette and Crowley insured a mass turnout. The "famous caterer of Opelousas" was in charge of the menu at the Crowley House. For three days, the band played while games of roulette, chuck-a-luck, and miniature lottery were played. A free barbecue capped each day's activity. The auction was a success and, only four months after the creation of the parish, the election was held. Using the argument that they were more centrally located, Crowley won the right to be called the Acadia parish seat.

In 1800, a Quaker man from Pennsylvania came to south Louisiana and laid out a town. It would become the parish seat eleven years later when the parish of St. Mary was formed. His name was Guinea Lewis, and he so admired Benjamin Franklin that he named the town after him.

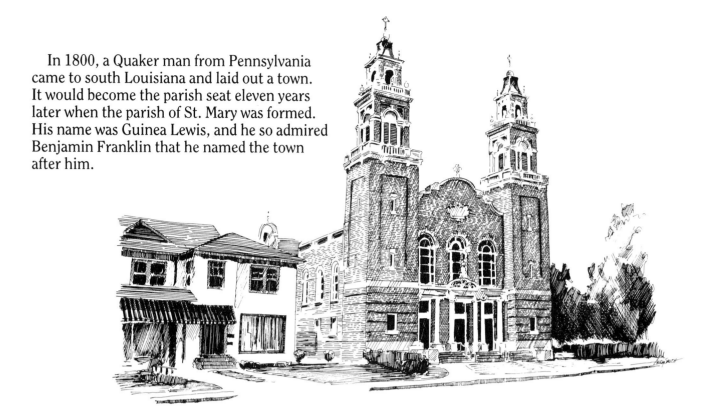

Plantations, sugar cane and the Bayou Teche played key roles in Franklin's development. It grew because it was the port of entry for the Teche country. It was the center of trade for a large area until the railroad was built and New Orleans and Galveston started receiving this commerce directly.

Being a port city was not without its difficulties. During the Yellow Fever epidemic, around the middle of the century, the people of Franklin forced all steamers coming from New Orleans to stop for a period of quarantine. One Captain, choosing to ignore the restriction, churned right past the station stop. Word traveled faster than the steamer and, as he rounded the bend, he saw what seemed like the entire town descending toward him. The courthouse bell could be heard ringing in the distance as the townsfolk, armed with muskets, cannon and pitchforks, lined the shore. The message seemed clear and he was finally persuaded to obey the restrictions.

Franklin

The need for expansion finally became necessary due to the increasing population. The cemetery markers were moved to a new site and a market built on the old graveyard. Banshees and ghosts were seen by some of the town folk, and the evening hours usually saw this area deserted. But the expansion also brought lumber and brick industries, an ice plant, banks and sugar refineries. The churches and schools completed the picture as Franklin became an active and prosperous place to live.

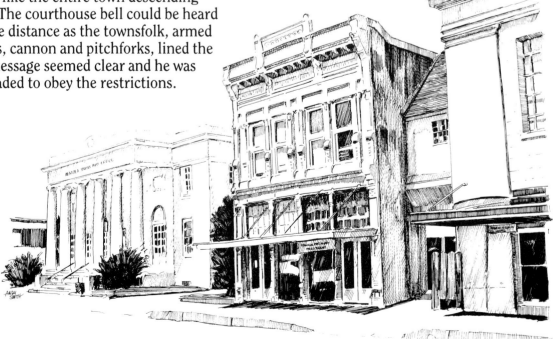

St. Mary Parish/FRANKLIN 83

Jennings

Jennings McComb was the engineer for the Southern Pacific Railroad, and he laid the tracks here. Soon a small settlement emerged. It grew rapidly, but not in proportion to the large influx of people it was experiencing. It was to become a supply town, a gathering place for the northern farmers seeking homesteads. Here they stayed until their homes could be located, and it was here that they returned when supplies had to be restocked. Jennings had become a town of tradesmen.

The Industrial era, started by the first Louisiana oil well, began another period of migration in the early 1900s. This growing number of people, tiring of the long ride to Lake Charles for justice, demanded a new Parish. Finally after 10 years of constant pressure, a new parish was established. As the leader of the fight, Jennings thought it should be named the parish seat; the people of Welsh, using the more centrally located theme, disagreed. The ensuing battle generated much excitement. Welsh cleared the land for the expected courthouse and, as the votes were being tallied, one long time Jennings resident died of a heart attack before he could hear the final count that placed the Parish seat in Jennings by only 79 votes.

One final conflict arose around the naming of the Parish. The honor of selecting the name was given to the Daughters of the Confederacy. They chose, to the dismay of the large number of northern settlers, the name Jefferson Davis. Shortened to Jeff Davis Parish, the parish seat remains today in the railroad town called Jennings.

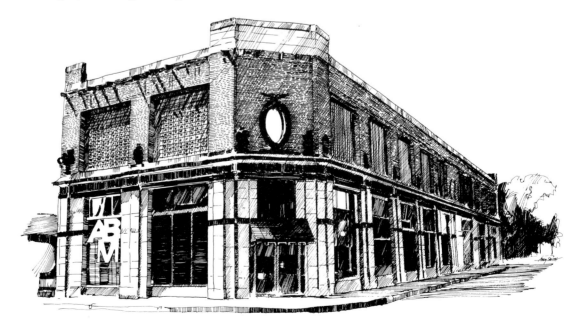

Jefferson Davis Parish/JENNINGS 85

Where the Vermilion River would no longer support their boats, the smugglers stopped. They waited to trade with the Indians, trappers and the few scattered farmers of the area. Here, where transportation had come to a halt, a small trading settlement sprang up. It was called La Petit Manchac.

It was a slow growing community, but not without its attractions. One was the establishment run by the man and wife who served the best fried chicken in the area. Everyday their place was crowded and there seemed to be no end to their supply of chickens. His secret was discovered early one morning. Attaching a piece of corn to a pin, he would throw it among the wandering chickens that belonged to his neighbors. When the corn was swallowed, the chicken would be hauled in, and the process repeated until he had his daily quota. Soon the area became known as Pin Hook. The Spring of 1863 saw a desperate battle between Southern General Taylor and the Federal forces, under General Banks, at this place called Pin Hook.

In the 1880s, traveling priests referred to the village as St. Jean. This was about two miles from the settlement at Pin Hook. On lands donated by Jean Mouton, a church was established and dedicated as "L'eglise St. Jean du Vermilion." With the church, people settled nearby and the growing settlement was called St. Jean by some, Vermilionville by most. The church soon became the focal point for social and religious activities. More families flocked to the area. The parish seat was moved from Pin Hook to Vermilionville as it became larger. Finally its name was changed to Lafayette, in honor of the man for whom the parish had been named.

Lafayette

The Old Spanish Trail winds its way beside the clear lake, which was first traveled by the Indians, then the Spanish Conquistadores and then the French Adventurers. Finally herds of as many as 5000 cattle were seen swimming across the Calcasieu River as the Texas cowboys followed this trail, now called the Beef Trail or the Old Opelousas Road.

Settling on this road next to the lake, came the New Orleans Spaniard, Carlos Salia. He later changed his name to Charles Sallier and built a home. To his neighbors he became known as Mr. Charles, and the lake he lived on as "Charles Lake." Continuing troubles on the border resulted in the building of a Fort on the banks of the lake.

It was given the name Cantonment Atkinson, and was later sold to Thomas Bilbo. Commanding a superb view of the lake and river, Bilbo used these structures as a base from which he surveyed the Parish of Calcasieu. He also entertained friends who were traveling the Old Spanish Trail, among them Sam Houston and Santa Ana.

During the time of the Border dispute, Easterners came from Mississippi to settle. As their numbers grew, they started to think about becoming organized. It was a two week ride to the parish seat in Opelousas, through less than friendly countryside. Finally the Imperial Calcasieu Parish was formed and Marion became the Parish seat. Selected because it was located on the Texas trail, it remained small and relatively inactive, with only a courthouse and jail located there. It was not until Jacob Ryan Jr. took the matter in his own hands that the Parish seat was moved to his town of Charleston, located on the lake. By ox-wagons, through the woods, the courthouse and jail were moved and relocated on the square of ground now occupied by the Calcasieu Parish Courthouse, in the town now known as Lake Charles.

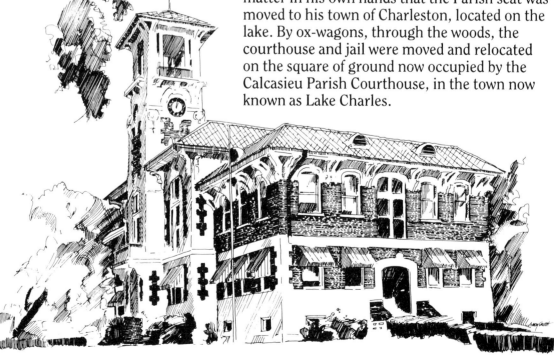

Louisiana Proud

Lake Charles

Morgan City

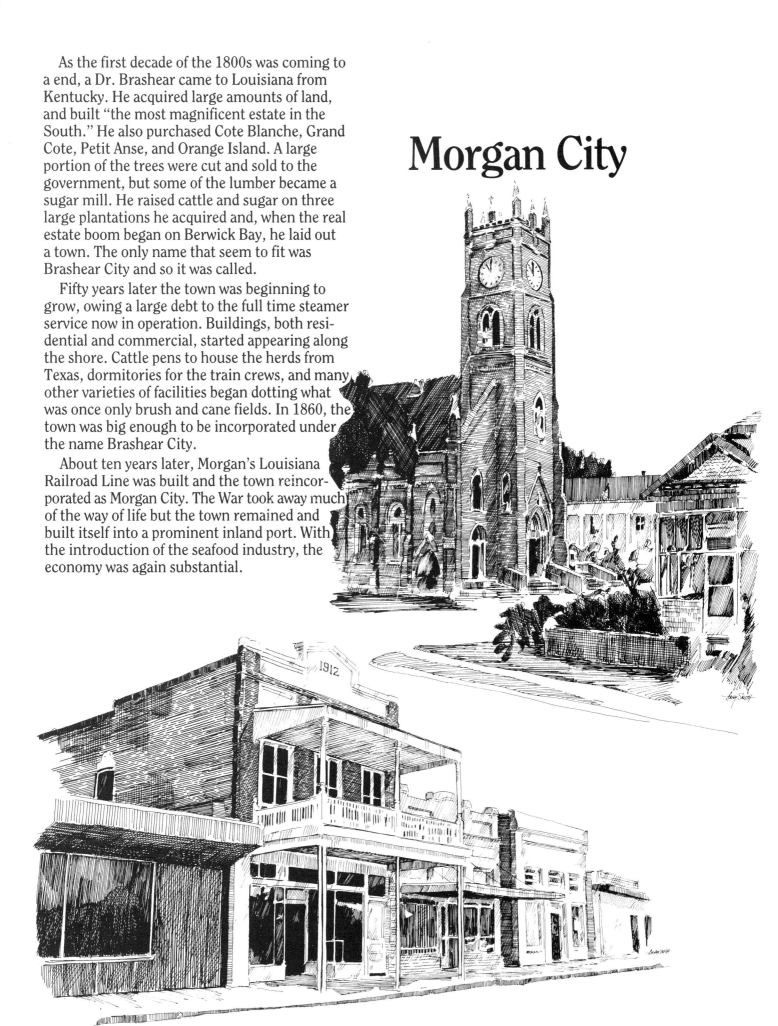

As the first decade of the 1800s was coming to a end, a Dr. Brashear came to Louisiana from Kentucky. He acquired large amounts of land, and built "the most magnificent estate in the South." He also purchased Cote Blanche, Grand Cote, Petit Anse, and Orange Island. A large portion of the trees were cut and sold to the government, but some of the lumber became a sugar mill. He raised cattle and sugar on three large plantations he acquired and, when the real estate boom began on Berwick Bay, he laid out a town. The only name that seem to fit was Brashear City and so it was called.

Fifty years later the town was beginning to grow, owing a large debt to the full time steamer service now in operation. Buildings, both residential and commercial, started appearing along the shore. Cattle pens to house the herds from Texas, dormitories for the train crews, and many other varieties of facilities began dotting what was once only brush and cane fields. In 1860, the town was big enough to be incorporated under the name Brashear City.

About ten years later, Morgan's Louisiana Railroad Line was built and the town reincorporated as Morgan City. The War took away much of the way of life but the town remained and built itself into a prominent inland port. With the introduction of the seafood industry, the economy was again substantial.

Louisiana Proud

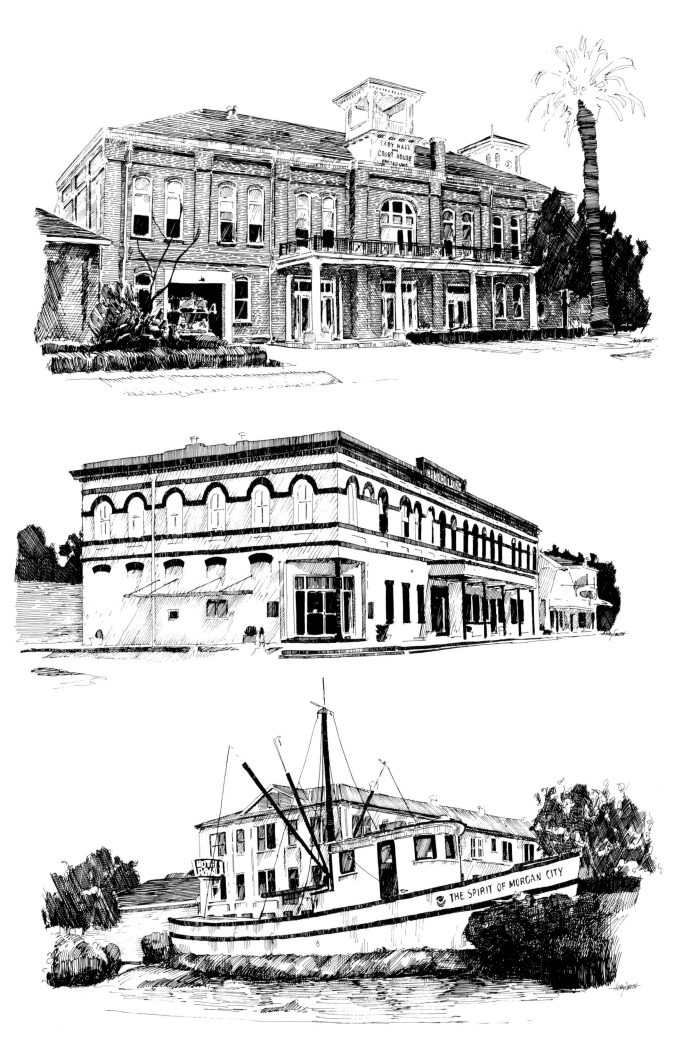

St. Mary Parish/MORGAN CITY 91

New Iberia

It seems strange that it was the Spanish who developed this area of French Louisiana. Leaving New Orleans, the small group of Spaniards, under the command of Bouligny, turned west at Bayou Plaquemine. They followed the bayou until it emptied into the Atchafalaya Basin. Making their way up the Bayou Teche, they finally stopped at what seemed a strategic spot and started a small trading settlement. The area was beautiful and it reminded them of their homeland of Iberia, where flowers grew in abundance. They named it New Iberia.

Six months later they were six feet under water. Gathering what they could salvage they left the area, which is now Charenton, and traveled twenty miles up the bayou to the next bend in the Teche. On a slight bluff they settled and built homes, this time nine feet above the ground. That same year, Spain declared war on Great Britain and all the new settlements were left with no assistance from their Mother country. By 1880, a year later, with no guidance, the people became independent and started refusing to take orders, and in fifteen years Spanish rule was gone forever.

It was an area filled with enormous potential, however, it failed to grow. It drifted into becoming cattle country and emerged as a large shipping point which provided beef for the large plantations along the Mississippi. At the time the Acadians were filtering down to the area, New Iberia was still a part of St. Martin Parish. St. Martinville, the parish seat, demanded tribute from all the other towns in the parish. With no reinvestment for civic improvements, the other towns remained at the "no growth" level.

Eighty years later, the new parish of Iberia was formed and New Town, as it was sometimes called, became the seat of government. The discovery of salt, a larger, deeper river port with easier access to the world, fertile soil, the introduction of the railroad and the determination of the people pushed the town of New Iberia ahead of its once more influential neighbors.

CENTRAL SECTION

Alexandria
Rapides Parish

Bunkie
Avoyelles Parish

Colfax
Grant Parish

DeRidder
Beauregard Parish

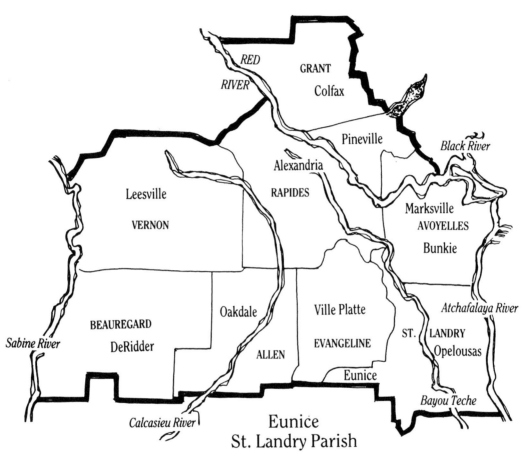

Eunice
St. Landry Parish

Leesville
Vernon Parish

Marksville
Avoyelles Parish

Oakdale
Allen Parish

Opelousas
St. Landry Parish

Pineville
Rapides Parish

Ville Platte
Evangeline Parish

Louisiana Proud

Alexandria

The Red River has been a key artery in the discovery and exploration of this vast new land called Louisiana. The earliest explorers penetrated her length via its liquid path. The obstacle which caused much concern, located about midway between New Orleans and Natchitoches, was the churning waters caused by the rocks in the river. These rapids caused the boats to be unloaded and carried across a stretch of land, then reloaded again before travel could continue. Oftentimes cargoes never reached the other end of the rapids, as bandits made this their home. A small fort called Poste du Rapides was built and a town was begun.

Indians, French soldiers turned planters, Spanish traders and Acadians all gathered at "Les Rapides." Later they were joined by the Anglo-Saxons from the eastern seaboard. In 1810, on lands owned by Alexander Fulton, a town was laid out and named Alexandria for his infant daughter who died the same year. In ten years, Alexandria became a busy shipping and trading center fueled by the increasing numbers of steamships which arrived daily. The lumber from the nearby forest was stripped and sent to New Orleans for the building of that town. In its place were planted fields of cotton and sugar cane. The first railroad tracks west of the Mississippi were laid in the area and a ferry driven by blind horses kept constant touch with its sister city across the river, Pineville.

Louisiana Proud

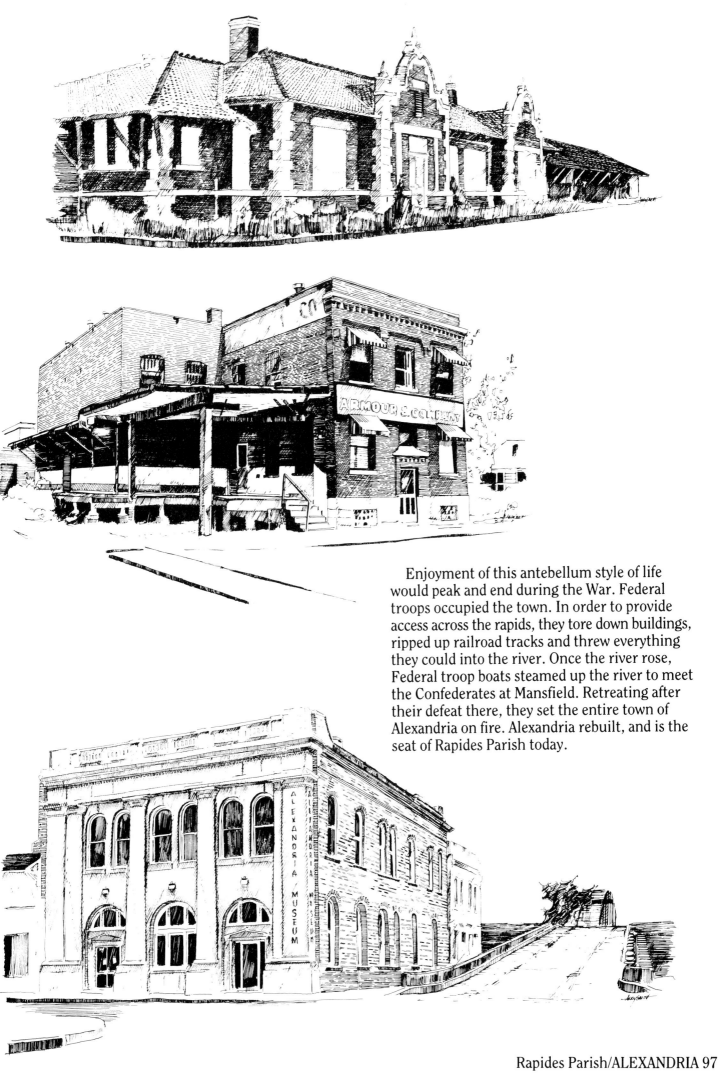

Enjoyment of this antebellum style of life would peak and end during the War. Federal troops occupied the town. In order to provide access across the rapids, they tore down buildings, ripped up railroad tracks and threw everything they could into the river. Once the river rose, Federal troop boats steamed up the river to meet the Confederates at Mansfield. Retreating after their defeat there, they set the entire town of Alexandria on fire. Alexandria rebuilt, and is the seat of Rapides Parish today.

This land called Irion was owned by only a few.

It was first settled by Major Irion, who fought in the War of 1812, and later by Samuel Hass, who captained a force of active Confederates. After acquiring large areas of land, they were content to farm them. Their first job was the clearing of the trees and cane. With no local markets for the timber it was just set ablaze. Life was constant year after year, although it was due to change radically.

In the late 1800s, Captain Haas gave the right of way through his lands to the Texas and Pacific Railway. A strip of businesses sprang up along the track with the depot in the center. Captain Haas was given the honor of naming the town. He had given his daughter a mechanical toy monkey and, as she was just starting to talk, all she could say was "bunkie." This became her nickname and the name chosen for the new depot.

Riding on the back of the railroad, Bunkie, the youngest town in the parish, soon became one of the largest. The surrounding towns began bringing their cotton here because shipment to market was faster. The steamboat era was over and to Bunkie came the treasure of commerce that once was others.

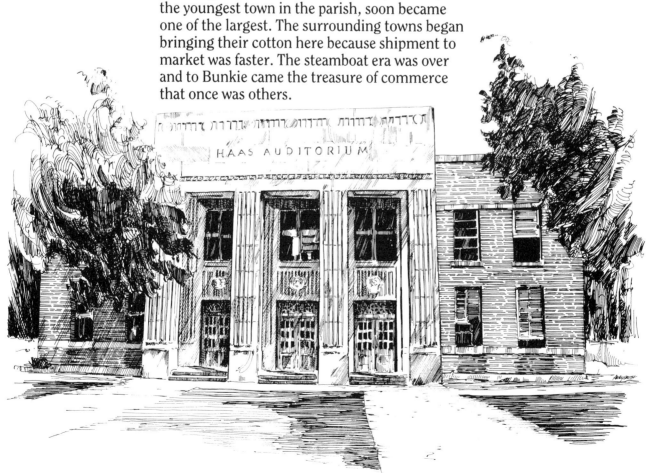

Louisiana Proud

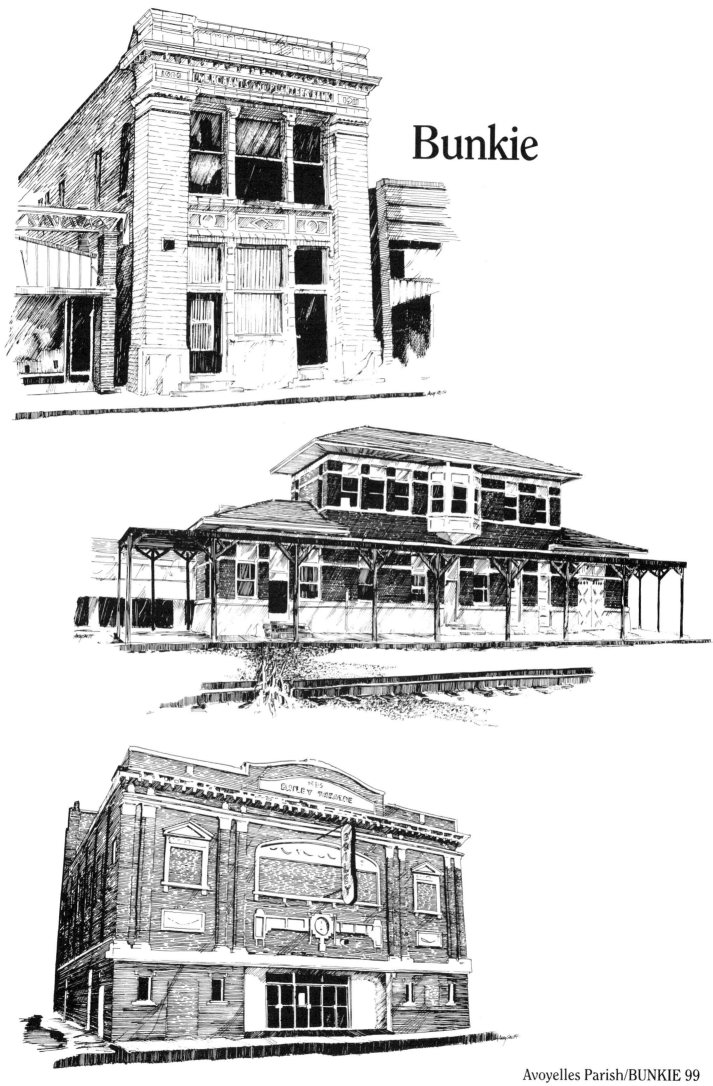

Bunkie

Colfax

Near the slowly running muddy waters, called the Red River, was the home of Meredith Calhoun. A cotton planter, whose plantation consisted of 14,000 acres and over 1000 slaves, he had built his home on the banks of the Rigolette de Bon Dieu. All the produce harvested in the area was brought to his dock for shipping. It was called Calhoun's Landing. After one of the periodic floods, Calhoun's Landing found itself on the Red River; the channel had changed and merged with the once quiet Rigolette.

The steamboats brought people, and the people meant more commerce and commerce generated prosperity, all at the doorstep of Mr. Calhoun's home. Calhoun's Landing was growing.

As the War came to an end and Reconstruction began, a new parish was created. It was named by the new rulers of the South in honor of President Ulysses S. Grant. Calhoun's Landing was made the parish seat and renamed for the new vice-president, Schuyler Colfax. It was the era of the Carpetbag and Scalawag rule, and Colfax was thrown into the middle of it. When elections were called, a band of 300 armed black men forced the white families to disband, pillaged the town, and killed those that resisted. By the time news of the killing of the Judge's young child, who was dumped in his yard, reached the outside world, an army had already been formed. The resulting conflict ended what had been called the Colfax Riots, as the slaves were either forced to flee or were killed in the ensuing battle. After the whiskey had taken control, the mob quickly overcame the guards and the forty or so prisoners were taken and hung en masse at the Oak which came to be known as the "Riot Tree."

With time, the coming of the sawmills and the railroad, Colfax returned to its normal life of the land.

Louisiana Proud

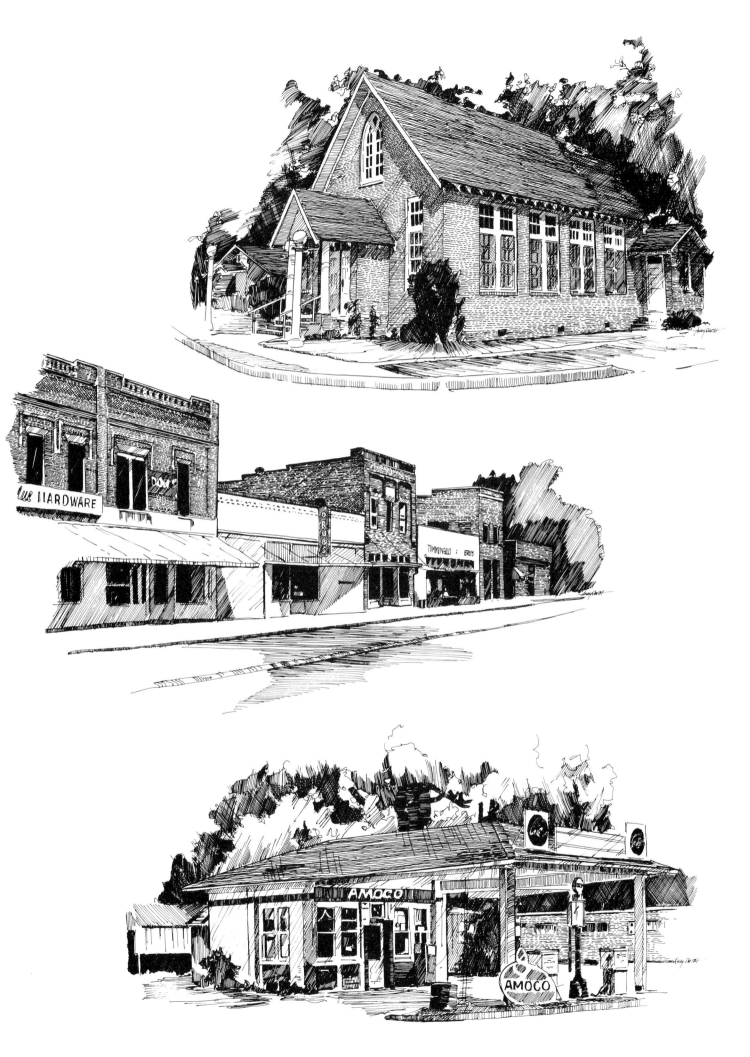

Grant Parish/COLFAX 101

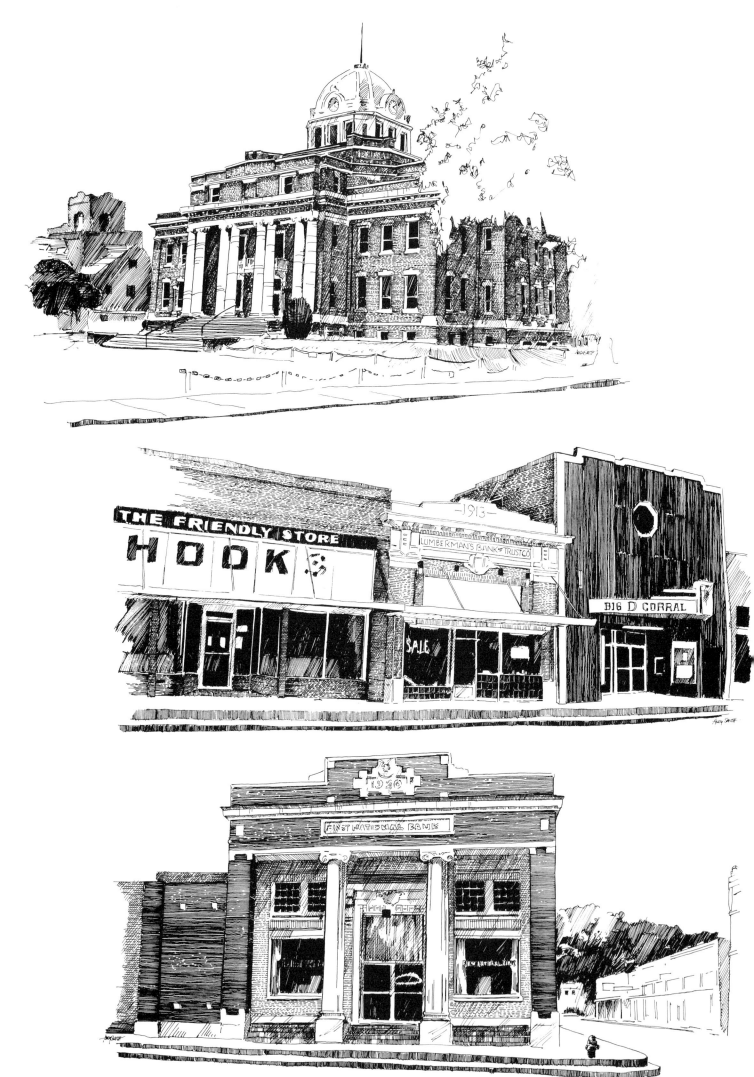

Louisiana Proud

Originally known as Schovall, it was changed to Miersburg when the post office was established. This town, which was once a part of the Imperial Calcasieu Empire, saw its name changed again to DeKidder, who was an official of the railroad, and then finally to DeRidder.

DeRidder has long been an important town in western Louisiana. First, it was a prosperous lumbering town with many sawmills. Then as the growing population led to the formation of Beaurgard Parish, new responsibilities were forced on her as the parish seat. The people sought legislative representation and dispensed justice to the outlaws and river pirates of the area.

As the population grew, stores, schools, churches and banks began to emerge to service them. After the trees were cut, these industrious people turned their energies toward the cutover land and produced various crops year after year.

The two railroad systems which transversed this section of Southwest Louisiana, known as the Highlands, did much to enhance the economy of the area by delivering the products of the sawmills and produce of the land to new markets, and insured the continued growth of DeRidder.

DeRidder

Open prairie land stretched as far as the eye could see. It was called Prairie Faque Taique and the few scattered settlers lived miles from each other. It was the early 1890s.

As he looked over the land, this man called C.C. Duson saw more than just empty prairie land. He envisioned a town and people. Finally, persuading Guy Fusilier to share his dream, he bought the land. Fusilier owned the only store in the area, so he was a natural to spread the word to travelers and also he acted as the agent for the project. It took several years before their plan could be implemented. But what a plan it was to be.

"A Great Auction" headlined the liberally placed advertisements in Mississippi, Texas, Louisiana and Alabama papers. Special excursion train schedules were announced. People were at the ready. It started raining on Sunday, continued Monday, and on Tuesday it poured. Many were kept away by the weather, but thousands came by train and at least fifteen hundred on foot or horseback. Wednesday was the first day of the Sale and people seemed determined to be present. The Crowley and Rayne bands played while the Auction in French and English started. Barbecue was the main course. In three days the Auction was over and a town had been born. It took only a few weeks for hotels, warehouses, and other stores to appear, and permanently change the look of this flat prairie land. Duson was given the honor of naming the town he had brought to life. He named it Eunice, after his wife.

Eunice

All through the swamp lay fallen trees. They signaled the start of the new industry, which would shortly bring wealth and destruction to the Parish of Vernon.

Leesville

The early pioneer would cut the large trees, trim them, and then cut others. He would do this for weeks, giving each his own distinguishing mark. Finally the rains would start and the real work began. As the water slowly filled the banks of the swamps, the logs became mobile. Floating his harvest to the river, he tied them together into a raft and floated them down river. Lumber had always been the incentive that drew the settler to Vernon Parish. It was a country for only the strongest of heart. Cutting, trimming, and manhandling impossible weights of massive trees for hours on end was the reward for reaching this land.

This was also the middle of the "Neutral Strip," and many an outlaw made a fortune robbing and killing the settlers and travelers passing through the raw natural wilderness.

A large settlement grew on the lands of Dr. Smart. At first there was only his office and a general mercantile store. Right before the turn of the century, the railroad came to Vernon Parish and the settlement and population grew rapidly. Soon it was the business center for a growing lumber industry. It consisted of three distinct districts, Old Town, New Town and Mill Town. Old Town was the business district consisting of a courthouse, a jail, churches, etc.

Dr. Smart's town, named by him, Leesville, in honor of General Robert E. Lee, flourished during the boom years of the lumber industry. Eventually it became the parish seat of government. When Vernon was stripped of 70% of its natural wealth, many of the smaller settlements faded from the landscape. Leesville remained, its forests returned, and this time managed to provide a constant source of revenue for its people. The activation of Fort Polk and its large payroll added to the prosperity of the area.

Louisiana Proud

Marksville

The white men were stealing the Redman's land!

During the late 1700s, a fort was established to protect the Indians from the growing numbers of settlers. These newcomers were the Acadians who had landed along the rivers. The daring ones moved inland to the lands of the Avoyelles Indians. One of the earliest was Marc Eliche, a merchant from France. Making friends with the Indians, he soon established a trading post near the fort. There he swapped furs and fish for New Orleans merchandise which was provided by the river steamers. As more settlers arrived in the area, his store inventory, as well as the quality of his merchandise, grew. Homes and other business establishments followed shortly. It was called Marc's Village. In time the name was changed to Marksville, and became the seat of government for the parish of Avoyelles.

Everything centered around the courthouse. Stores flanked every side and the number of tied-up horses indicated that this was the center of activity. Marksville grew, and throughout the state became known for its stores, hotels, and educational system. Fierce competition among the many store owners kept the citizens well equipped with the latest of everything. You could even have a drink with ice in it if you could afford the cost, as ice had to be shipped from New Orleans in kegs insulated with saw dust. Small earthen levees enabled the citizens to go from one place to another, as this prairie land often retained its water and turned to mud. Dancing and horse racing were the major social events of the day. Improvements were slow to come. However, the courthouse and the shipping empire built by its merchants guaranteed continued growth for the town of Marksville.

Two miles southeast of its present site, on a low area of land between the Calcasieu River and East Bay, lived William T. Dunn. He owned a grist mill, a cotton gin and a sawmill. In addition, he was the Postmaster and he called the area Bay. Dunn was given a patent for 160 acres of land which he split with the town. Bay was moved and took the name Dunnsville.

Oakdale

Dunnsville, located amidst the great timber stands of long leaf pine forests, began to develop a large lumber industry. This brought the railroad through the town and stimulated even more growth. Telegraph and Express offices, good schools and several fine mercantile establishments were the result of the new riches that the lumber industry brought to the four hundred people living there.

The large Live Oaks, that once shaded Dunnsville, so impressed a team of surveyors that they changed the name for the third time to Oakdale. The Oakdale Post Office came into existence in the late 1890s and though the Oaks have been cut for the expansion of the town, the name remains.

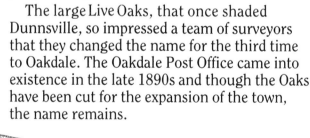

Louisiana Proud

Opelousas

There was no place to preach in the "ungodly city" of New Orleans for a new Methodist preacher in 1806. The new settlements in the Opelousas country surely had more need. Upon arrival, he found that three-quarters of the people spoke French, owned large herds and rarely came to town. The others were Indians. Disappointed, he was forced to remain there, where the Sabbath was spent in frolicking and gambling, until the swamps receded.

He had come to a French trading post where whiskey and guns were traded for furs and skins. Called the "Poste des Opelousas," it was established to instill fear in the Indians and protect the emigrations of new French settlers. By the time Louisiana had become part of the United States, the settlement was the head of government for the larger County of Opelousas. Cattle, cotton and eventually sugar were the main produce of the country. One of the new families was called Bowie. Jim and his brother spent their childhood and were married here. Later Jim would become an adventurer who mingled with men like Lafitte and Crockett.

It remained, for a long time, a frontier town. Indians were more numerous than the slaves. It was from them that the town took its name. They were called "black legs" because of the paint they used to distinguish their tribe from others. They were the Opelousas Indians.

During the Civil War, Opelousas, for a time, became the Capital of the State. Its people had established a thriving community despite its frontier location. The Capital remained here only shortly, as the Yankees followed it from Baton Rouge. When the smoke had cleared, the Capital was in Shreveport and Opelousas was soon to face what was termed " the Dark Days" of Reconstruction.

Opelousas had grown because of the richness of the soil, the railroad and the spirit of its people. When the War and Reconstruction were over, the parts were still there and the town was rebuilt.

Pineville

The same rapids which led to the establishment of Alexandria on the west bank, nurtured a settlement on the east bank, which in time became Pineville. The fluctuating Red River and rapids created the need for the establishment of a fort to protect the cargoes which had to be portaged overland. Pineville became a trading post which serviced the farmers and traders east of the Red River.

The river was both a blessing and a curse to the city. It was hard to remember the good times brought by the steamers and river traffic when the town was under water. The little town continued to flourish, however. Its stores, churches, tavern and brewery were encouraged by the trade and commerce of the river. Life for the most part seemed good until the spring of 1860 and its men left the fields for the battleground. The town suffered along with Alexandria with the occupation of the Federals. As the War ended, Reconstruction began and Pineville grew very little. The people became craftsmen and it was not until the introduction of the railroad that its commerce increased to any extent. The ferry would be replaced by a bridge and the communities of Alexandria and Pineville would enter the twentieth century together.

Louisiana Proud

Was the Major preparing for the day when Napoleon retook his former possessions in America, or was this just the place where the old soldier finally settled? The mystery remains, but the fact is that Marcelin Garand, an Adjutant Major in Napoleon's army who had lost his sight on the Battlefields of Russia, was an early settler on this flat prairie land. He entertained the frequent travelers at his tavern with stories of Napoleon and the war. Located on the main road between Alexandria and Opelousas, Garand remained an influential force in this tiny community until his death in the 1850s.

When Josephine, whose beautiful hair touched the floor, was discovered with her lover in the garden, by her brother, a duel ensued. When it was over, the lover was dead. The King's law of dueling was violated and the dead man's family was seeking revenge. De Vidrine took his wife, family and Josephine and fled. They came from France to the prairies and to the town of the blind soldier.

The French speaking town on the edge of the large meandering flat Mamou Prairie was named by its inhabitants. They called their town "Flat Town," or Ville Platte in their native language. With a population which consisted of soldiers of Napoleon's old army, members of Lafitte's pirate gang and hundreds of energetic French, the town grew. Almost fifty years later, they made such a demand for a closer seat of justice that a new parish was created. Thus was born Evangeline Parish.

Ville Platte

Eunice, Mamou, Ville Platte and Pine Prairie each wanted the seat of government in their town and tried to outdo each other with concessions and inducements. The vote was tallied and Ville Platte became the Parish Seat. It was not without dissension however, as Eunice, declaring foul, decided to remain in St. Landry Parish.

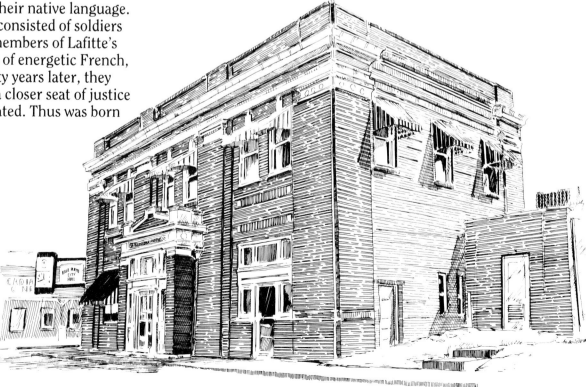

Arcadia

Located in the hills of Bienville Parish and named during the excavations of the ancient cities of Greece, Arcadia echoes the Classical theme. In the days of Homer, a town existed in the mountains between Sparta and Athens; it was called Arcadia. In the middle eighteen hundreds, a small sleepy village sprang to life between Sparta in Bienville Parish and Athens, located in the neighboring parish of Claiborne. Its people called it Arcadia.

Visitors were frequent, but they stayed only long enough for the horses to be changed on the stagecoach line from Monroe to El Paso.

The coming of the Iron Horse changed all this into an era of rapid growth. Now Arcadia was a meeting place for the farmers to ship their produce to larger markets. Businesses, stores, churches and schools began to appear. As the population grew, the seat of government was moved from Sparta. The establishement of a Post Office, Bank and the Arcadia Male and Female College turned this primitive stagecoach stop into a thriving community.

J.B.WHITE CO

Sitting on a bluff, overlooking the Red River, a tiny trading settlement had been established. It consisted of two small stores, one called Cane's and the other Bennett's. Bennett's Bluff, the first name by which the sleepy community was called, was directly across the river from the long established town of Shreveport. All commerce was carried on there. Until the Vicksburg, Shreveport and Pacific Railroad spanned the Red River, all travel was by ferry. The name was changed to Cane City, but the shadow of Shreveport continued to blot out any real growth or progress.

In the 1840s, General Pierre Evatiste John Baptiste Bossier, a congressman from Natchitoches, pushed the Bill through the legislature to create a new Parish. In the 1880s, a vote was taken for the removal of the parish seat, which was then in Bellevue, to either Cane City or Benton. Cane City won the election, but a constitutional flaw was discovered, allowing the seat of government to be moved to Benton.

It was almost sixty years after the creation of the parish that the town would be large enough to be incorporated. It took the name Bossier City, after the name of the parish. Shreveport still is the dominant city of the north but Bossier City has made its own progress and continues to play an important role in the history of the state. In 1951, the population having increased beyond 15,000, Governor Earl K. Long, by proclamation, made Bossier City a city.

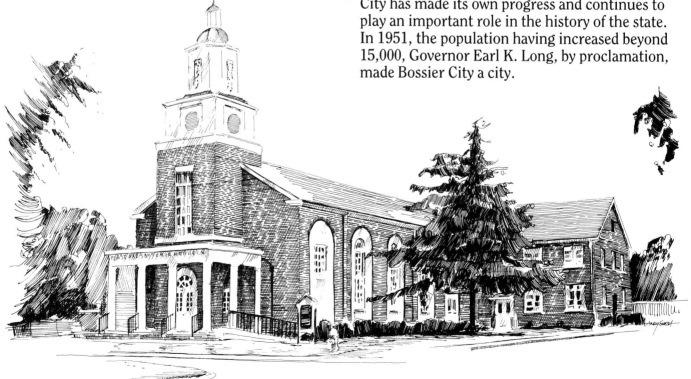

Louisiana Proud

Bossier City

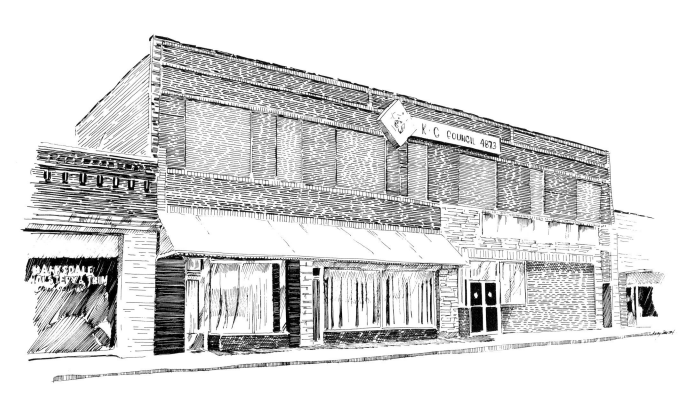

Coushatta

The ferry had just departed when the man in black reached the river bank. He dismounted reaching for his rifle, his long black coat almost brushing the ground. He walked slowly toward the blacksmith. A short conversation with the smith, revealed that it was Twitchell and King, who were the passengers on the ferry. Quick steps took the stranger to the edge of the Red River and as the blacksmith watched in horror, he opened fire.

King was dead immediately. Twitchell, receiving wounds that eventually led to the amputation of both arms, sold his property and moved to New Orleans. Justice had been quickly dispensed to the infamous leaders of Reconstruction. The bloody times of the Coushatta Riots were over.

Louisiana Proud

This event put an end to the corrupt and extravagant carpetbag rule during Reconstruction and brought peace back to the location known to the Indians as "White Reed-Brake" or Coushatta Chute.

Coushatta is now located one and one-half miles from the original town site, then known as Springville. The inconveniences of hauling freight and the improved river transportation overcame the Springville's residents fear of the marshes and germ carrying mosquitoes. Fire, floods, river changes and even the War could not discourage the people of Coushatta. Stores and churches sprang up. When the town was selected as the Red River Parish seat of government, the people built a magnificent courthouse, complete with clock tower, where justice was quickly and efficiently dispensed.

Homer

As the ashes were still cooling at the smoldering courthouse in Athens, a movement was gaining impetus. The population had moved and the idea for a new town and parish seat, more centrally located, took hold. On a gently rising plateau, between the D'Arbonne and Corni Creeks, overlooking the surrounding countryside, a site was selected. When the land was donated, the vote to move was unanimous; Homer was born.

The natural landscape soon became the victim of the ax and the builder, as more and more people flocked to the new Courthouse site. The first home served as the chapel for the first sermon. The judge, lawyers, and clerks stayed across the street from the clapboard shanty which served as the Courthouse. Homer grew up fast. Buildings were erected almost before the tree stumps were removed. A new Courthouse was built, torn down because of cracks, and built again. The modern Claiborne House Hotel was erected north of the Courthouse. Building continued at a feverish pace and the people continued to arrive. This activity was stalled and a gradual decline set in as the men went to War.

It was the Christmas season; things were returning to normal. The War had been over for ten years and the men and the businesses had returned.

Fire bells, not sleigh bells, awoke the towns citizens at two A.M. on the morning of the twenty-second. The fire which had started in the south section of town burned out of control. It ran quickly through the wood frame buildings until it finally came up against the two story brick wall of McCrainies' store. A giant town effort and a wind change finally checked the fire before the entire town was consumed.

The citizens, dead tired, decided to wait until after Christmas to start the rebuilding. They awoke to two feet of snow on the twenty-sixth, and when it finally stopped three days later, many of the weakened fire-swept buildings were crushed by the weight of the snow. Heartbroken, they set about the task of building their town again. The business section slowly started to grow and with the completion of the railroad, Homer soon regained its former elegance.

Claiborne Parish/HOMER 127

Jonesboro

Who killed the sheriff?

From out of the darkness a bullet struck him dead as he was escorting a shackled prisoner from the train. The mystery remains. This wilderness, which concealed many of the lawless men of the frontier, had taken the life of its pioneer man of the law. His name was Jones.

Fifty years earlier another man named Jones and his family came to these same forests to farm. It was no easy task, as the fields had to be cleared of the useless pine forests. He was the first to settle here, and as others came and made their homes, a small community developed. Officially called Macedonia, after the small Baptist church, it became more commonly known as Coon Town by the local residents because of the number of raiding raccoons in the area. When the railroad was routed through this settlement it was named Jonesboro. Some say it was in honor of the first family; others, for the slain sheriff.

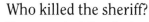

To whomever the honor belongs, it was a big
one, because by now Jonesboro had a sawmill
and people were staying and building substantial
structures. The railroad also brought the parish
seat. The records from Vernon were moved here,
as were most of the people who also brought
their businesses with them to this new capital
of Jackson Parish. Once a farming community,
then a booming lumber town, Jonesboro remains
today the seat of parish government.

In the 1840s, two hundred dollars and forty-eight cents bought a quarter section of timbered hill land in the heart of DeSoto Parish. It grew into a town where large trees shaded wide streets and spacious mansions, creating an antebellum atmosphere. Named after a Scottish hero, the Earl of Mansfield, the settlement became the parish seat and played an important part in the history of Louisiana.

It was in the eastern part of town that the Mansfield Female College, a leader in the education of women, was located. Education was interrupted during the War when the College structures became home and hospital to the Confederate soldiers.

It was here under a large spreading river oak that Confederate Generals Taylor and Mouton planned their defense against the invading Federal Army. A bloody battle ensued that saw the end of General Banks' Red River Campaign. When the Confederates stood their ground and defeated the Yankees, Banks' plan to capture the river towns, including Shreveport, and use this area as a landing place for the invasion of Texas was forgotten, as his remaining army battled its way north. At the end of the War, Mansfield returned to its life as a farming and lumber community.

It was the Mansfield Railway and Transportation Company that opened new markets for the town. Even the explosion of the locomotive that sent bodies flying and wrecked the depot did little to stop its steady growth as the city of dominance in DeSoto Parish.

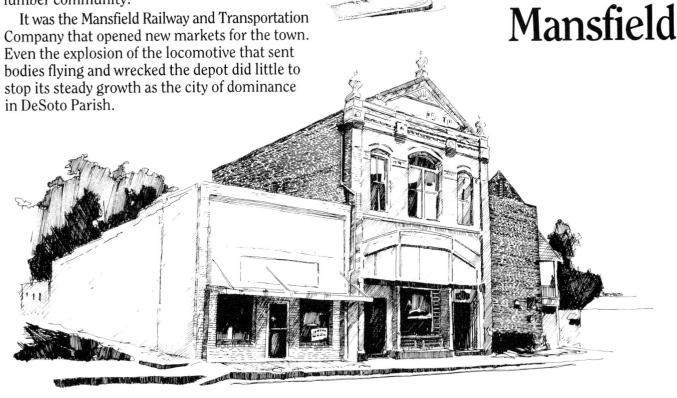

Mansfield

The dispute between French Louisiana and Spanish Texas over who owned a strip of land between the Sabine River and the town of Natchitoches resulted in the creation of "the Neutral Strip." Long a haven for killers, robbers and cut-throats, it was here, safe from the law, while waiting for his army to assemble, that the black hearted Aaron Burr finalized his plans for the establishment of a Western Empire of which he would be king.

Many

William Mains was the first to come with the intention of staying. He settled the plantation which eventually became a town. This was 1830 and he was alone, except for the Indians and wild beasts who watched him from the dense cane as he hacked out a spot for his family's cabin.

Later came John Baldwin, who sought the frontier life and its wilderness. His hotel/tavern became known as Baldwin's Store and later the parish seat. It was located on the main Natchitoches and San Antonio highway, and several miles from the only bastion of justice and safety, Fort Jesup. Although buildings were being built, it was not until a forty acre donation around Baldwin's Store that the town officially had any land of its own. Taking the name of Many, after one of the officers at Fort Jesup, it retained much of its Spanish character.

Until the establishment of the railroad, the merchants received their goods from New Orleans via the Red River Steamboats. Unloaded at Grand Encore, they were then freighted to Many by wagons. The railway also put an end to the mail rider and stagecoach lines. With no rush to settle, and situated on rolling hills in pine forests, Many has become a splendid town which belies the hostile territory from which it emerged.

Louisiana Proud

Minden

Louisiana Proud

Until the early 1800s, this was Indian land; the only whites seen here were a few hardy trappers and hunters. A man named Alden and another named Fields dared to leave the safety of the river settlements and to build homes here. It took almost seven years before other families started slowly drifting here to settle. Still it was another thirty years before a town was organized.

Charles Veeder erected the first building and launched a real estate promotion that would give life to the new town. As businessmen built stores and homes, a central water well was also being dug. The early settlers dredged the canals and bayous of the area to increase the river trade. The log jam below Shreveport caused many channels to be formed. Travel up the Red River had to be detoured through these lakes and bayous. Veeder's settlement was on one of these bayous. He had picked his location well. Named after his parent's birthplace in Germany, this town called Minden prospered.

Still a part of Claiborne Parish, Veeder pushed for the changing of the parish seat and established the Minden Academy, which later was divided into The Minden Male Academy and The Minden Female Academy. Veeder was discouraged when he could not bring the seat of government to Minden so he packed and left for the gold fields of California. A year later, when the new parish of Webster was created, his wish was fulfilled, and Minden was named the parish seat. The merchants and town prospered until an intruder stole 3000 annual bales of cotton. The new threat was the railroad. Some say a few of the older families were rude to the railroad officials and, when the tracks were completed five miles south, Minden lost another 5000 bales.

A feeder line built with the town's own money restored Minden to its former position. Main street still is paved of brick and the atmosphere of dignity and tranquility is like a breath of yesteryear.

It was the adventurer/explorer, Louis St. Denis, who explored the Great Red River Valley in this new Louisiana Country. His goal was to make friends with the Indians and to establish a permanent colony. He traveled up the Red River until he encountered the massive log jam called the Great Raft, which blocked the river to Shreveport, and caused him to stop. There he made friends with the tribe called the Natchitoches. With further boat passage impossible, he established a garrison on the banks of the Red River on the same camp grounds as the Indians. The construction of the warehouses was the beginning of the first permanent settlement in the New Lands.

Natchitoches

The trade between the Indians and French was enhanced when St. Denis and his Indian friends helped the Spanish build a fort some fifteen miles to the west.

Natchitoches was the westernmost outpost in America and rapidly became one of the country's most important trading posts. It also became the point of departure for all the adventuresome heading west. Military men and pioneers were often last seen here before entering the area called "No Man's Land." When the first steamboats docked, they found wharves bulging with silver, furs and skins waiting. Natchitoches soon became a booming port city. Even the removal of the Great Raft could not slow the city's growth. All it did was open new markets to its increasing number of merchants.

The spring floods were coming early this year and seemed heavier than usual. The normal precautions were being taken but no one could foresee the eventual result. Hidden by the muddy waters, the current eroded away the banks, with force enough to change the channel. When the waters subsided, the town was five miles from the main channel. With no avenue to the river, it became virtually a ghost town and left to die.

Left with a strip of pure water called the Cane River, Natchitoches retains its magic charm and heritage and is surrounded by fields of soybeans and cotton, forest and hills and crystal clear lakes.

Ruston

The building of the Vicksburg to Monroe railroad had been interrupted by the Civil War, and the tracks already laid had been torn up. After the war and the uneasy days of Reconstruction, building of the railroad was continued, although the route was somewhat altered. The discourteous attitude of a few rich people in Vienna and Minden toward the railroad resulted in the track being laid some four miles south, through the lands of Robert Russ.

Mr. Russ gave the lands for the right of way, and the railroad in turn built the depot. As the first locomotive chugged into town, the sign on the depot read Russ Town, in honor of Mr. Russ. A railroad engineer laid out the town, with wide streets around land also donated by Russ for the courthouse, school and cemetery.

Early interest and development was encouraged by a free train ride and barbecue, as Ruston advertised her wares. Each lot was $375 and each location was put in a hat and drawn. With the purchase of a city lot, came a free homesite.

When the parish seat was voted to be changed, almost the entire town of Vienna moved to Ruston. Things grew at a slow pace until the other north-south railroad came and cotton gins and sawmills sprang up. Still the expected boom did not develop. Ruston was left to grow quietly and peacefully, with social life centering around church sponsored oyster suppers, ice cream socials and an occasional visit to the Opera House for minstrel shows and to the Astor, now Dixie Theatre, for silent movies.

Louisiana Proud

Below the bluff, which was once the support for the tents of the Caddo Indians, was the end of river traffic on the River called Red. Spreading in all directions were nothing but marshy wet lands. There were no settlements, no people, only wilderness. At first it created no problem, as the small trading post community had no real population. Occasionally, the huge cattle herds from Texas crossed the bluff, as did some of the settlers in their wagons, going west. It was not until the people started to stay that the land to the south become desirable. The problem, however, seemed insurmountable.

For centuries it had been building, until it was now the biggest log jam in the country, stretching in excess of two hundred miles. It was given the name The Great Raft by the Caddos. Year after year, spring thaws sent high water and new debris down the river. It started piling up, each year claiming more and more of the river. Each year the blockage caused more flooding on both sides and more lands were denied to the hungry settlers. It had to be removed in order for the land to drain and there was only one man for the job-Captain Henry Miller Shreve.

With special boats he hauled all the timbers and forest debris out of the river, battling mosquitos, snakes and alligators the entire journey. At last the river was opened, the land drained and new settlers moved in. The big winner was the town which was then called Shreve's Town.

Shreveport

For years the area had been isolated because of the large log jam. Shreve's Town became the major town in this previous wilderness. Steamers were everyday occurrences at the docks, loading and unloading merchandise for the increased population of this rapidly growing frontier town. Growth was instantaneous. Shreve's Town had become Shreveport; its future would be secure, but not before it outlived its frontier reputation as a place where fraud, boundary disputes, Indian trouble and bloodshed were everyday events.

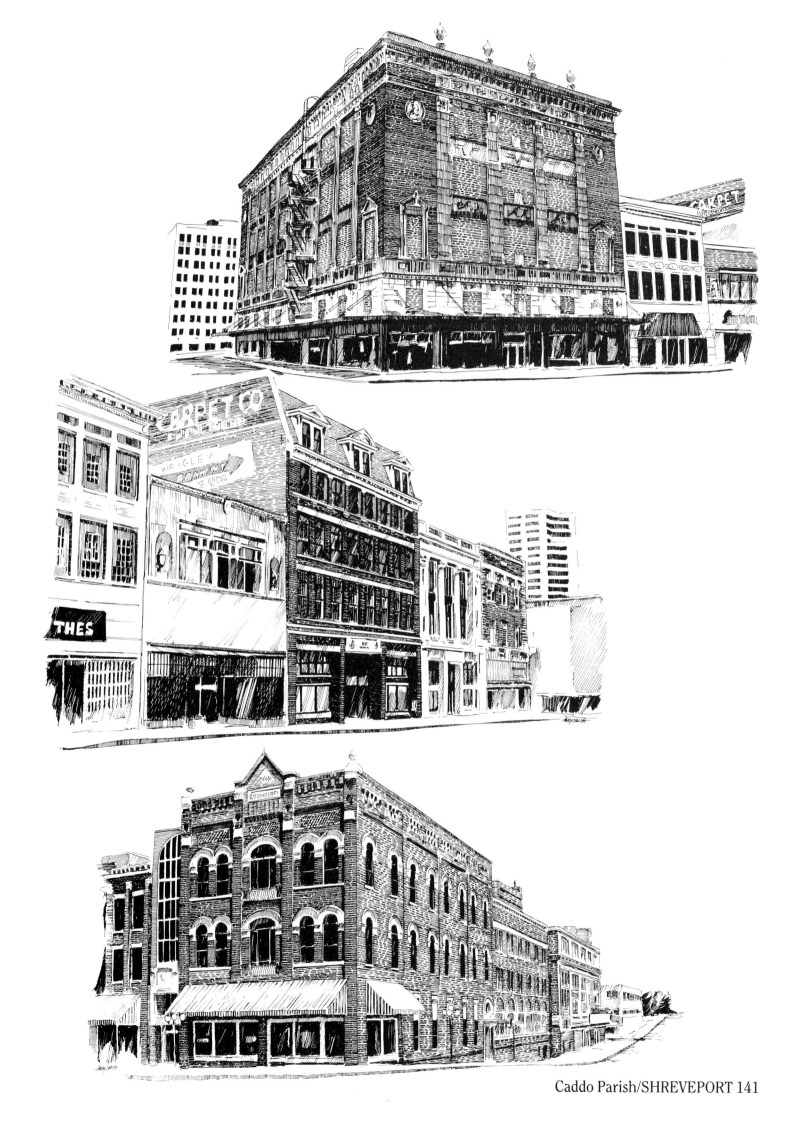

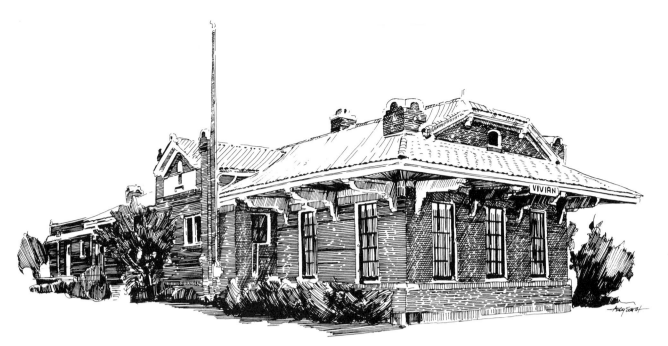

Vivian

Ten miles south of Arkansas and three miles east of Texas, in the land of the Caddo Indians, was a piece of land called "Terrapin Neck." Through it were laid the tracks of the railroad connecting Texarkana and Shreveport, and along the tracks was plotted a townsite. It was laid out by the Arkansas Townsite Company and given the name Vivian, in honor of a daughter of a railroad executive.

The industries of the area were farming and lumber. Saw mills and cotton gins dotted the landscape. Vivian enjoyed the services of its own doctor, whose home and drug store was the first two story structure erected. The railroad shipped large quantities of cotton and timber grown in the surrounding acres and was the reason for the town until the early 1900s.

Oil was discovered and a new rush of population flooded the area. It soon dominated the economy and when its famous Harrell No. 1 oil well blew and caught fire, leaving the countryside without nights for thirty days, the name of Vivian became recognized throughout the state. Oil is still produced and, along with the small farms and business establishments, continues to provide a pleasant life in this northern hill country.

Louisiana Proud

For years the red clay hills with its long leaf pine forest, thick canebrakes and fertile land lay dormant. Indians made periodic trips through the area to collect salt for their tribes. Occasionally a trapper or hunter would emerge from the woods, but it was not until the lands next to the river were populated that the settlers came here in any numbers.

It took until the 1840s before they came and settled in small communities, content to farm the land or hunt for their existence. One of these settlements came to called Winnfield, after an Alexandria lawyer named Walter O. Winn. When the parish was formed, Winnfield became the parish seat, although it would be almost fifty years before any boom in its economy would occur.

Winnfield

In the 1900s, the railroad provided the impetus. Ox-teams had been used to transport the logs from the giant forest. The railroad ended this when they located in the area. The lumber boom was on. The town grew fast with businesses locating around the courthouse square. Sometimes such a rapid growth draws hard people and Winnfield had its share. They worked hard during the day, and at night could be found on Tiger Street frequenting the many saloons and pool halls. Winnfield, in those early days, was raw and oftentimes violent. As more and more permanent buildings were completed, the town began to stabilize, and after the courthouse fire destroyed the records, the fighting was between the hordes of lawyers who congregated at the parish courthouse. One of the best known was Huey Long.

The Winnfield area has produced three governors of the state. (Huey Long, Earl Long, and O.K. Allen) and saw such notables as Sam Houston, Zachary Taylor, Robert E. Lee, Ulysses S. Grant and Jefferson Davis.

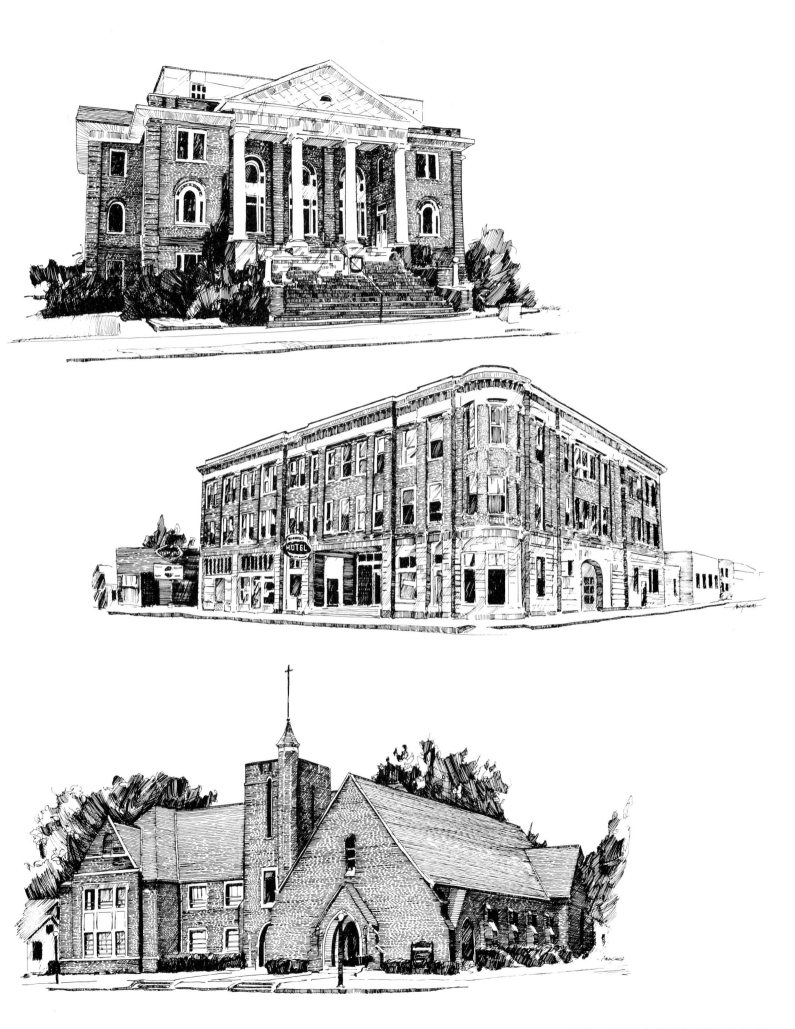

NORTHEAST SECTION

Bastrop
Morehouse Parish

Columbia
Caldwell Parish

Farmerville
Union Parish

Jena
LaSalle Parish

Jonesville
Catahoula Parish

Lake Providence
East Carroll Parish

Monroe
Ouachita Parish

Oak Grove
West Carroll Parish

Rayville
Richland Parish

St. Joseph
Tensas Parish

Tallulah
Madison Parish

Vidalia
Concordia Parish

Winnsboro
Franklin Parish

Farmerville
UNION

Bayou
D'Arbonne

Monroe
OUACHITA

Ouachita
River

Columbia
CALDWELL

Jena
LASALLE

Bastrop
MOREHOUSE

WEST
CARROLL

Oak
Grove

RICHLAND
Rayville

Bayou
Macon

FRANKLIN

Winnsboro

Tensas River

CATAHOULA
Jonesville

CONCORDIA

Vidalia

Black River

Lake
Providence

EAST
CARROLL

Tallulah
MADISON

St. Joseph

TENSAS

MISSISSIPPI RIVER

MISSISSIPPI

Louisiana Proud

Bastrop

Was he really a fraud, just an American adventurer who, in the disguise of a Dutch Baron, tricked the Baron de Corondelet into giving up large tracts of land, or was he for real?

The certainty is, that pleading his case for wanting to live in Spanish territory instead of the United States, he was granted large tracts of land in Northeast Louisiana with the requirement of bringing settlers to the area and establishing permanent communities. This was accomplished with the settlements at Mer Rouge and Point Jefferson.

As the population grew and the parish was being organized, friction between the two settlements over the parish seat occurred. When a compromise could not be reached, a new town was established and took its name from the original developer, The Baron de Bastrop. Laid out in 1846, the new parish seat consisted of 192 acres on the banks of Bayou Bartholemew. With the steamboats and later the railroads providing easy access for the cotton to get to market, it was not long before Bastrop became a prominent town in North Louisiana.

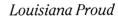

Morehouse Parish/BASTROP 149

Columbia

This location had seen such explorers as DeSoto and Bienville cross the river or pass close by. It was an early crossing for the Indians, then for the settlers on their way west. It was also here that Daniel Humphries built a log cabin and hunted bears. He called the place Columbia for a town in his native Carolina and it has remained a trading center for the area for over 150 years.

For almost twenty years, this small settlement, carved out of the wilderness on the west bank of the Ouachita, grew steadily. It was a good time, with the only inconvenience being the almost yearly overflows. In the middle of the 1800s, the area was almost decimated by Yellow Fever. It wiped out entire families. The cause was thought to be the early morning hours when the germ was thick in the air.

 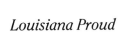

After the fever the town's growth regained its momentum, but fires were commonplace. Twenty years later every business establishment, except one, was destroyed. Everything was gone, but the people soon had new structures in their place and business was restored. This was a romantic time which saw the steamboat era in full swing. Captains and owners made their headquarters in and around Columbia and almost daily you could see the paddleboats Corona, Little Bob, America, Columbia, Ouachita or The Betsy Ann plying the river with cargos from here and there.

A dubious distinction was acquired one evening in the late 1800s when a group of men broke into the jail and lynched its prisoner. This act of violence gave Columbia the distinction of hanging a white man for killing a black. The people of Columbia were charged and they paid. The friends of the hanged man vowed to burn the town every ten years and they did. Twice! The rebuilding in brick finally brought an end to the fires, although from time to time an occasional fire did break out.

Farmerville

Living alone, trapping and tilling the soil, this man of the wilderness lived. He was John Honeycutt. It was from his Indian friends that he heard of a family with a house full of daughters. After short introductions he asked for one of their hands in marriage. The father quickly lined them up and Honeycutt took his pick, then disappeared into the forest.

It was on John Honeycutt's original land that the people, under the direction of W. Farmer, came to organize a parish government. Wanting to name the new parish seat Woodville for the president of the police jury, they finally settled on Farmerville after Mr. Wood's refusal.

Even through the hard days of Reconstruction the progressive spirit of the townspeople was evident. Modern structures, the Farmerville Institute and the only parish newspaper proved that. Farmerville grew with the age of the steamboats as people and goods continued to flow towards the town. Early evidence of its importance as a town can be seen when Henry Clay thought it important enough to make a speech here under an old oak which still stands today. Although the railroad ended the steamboat era, it opened new markets and spurred the town's growth even more.

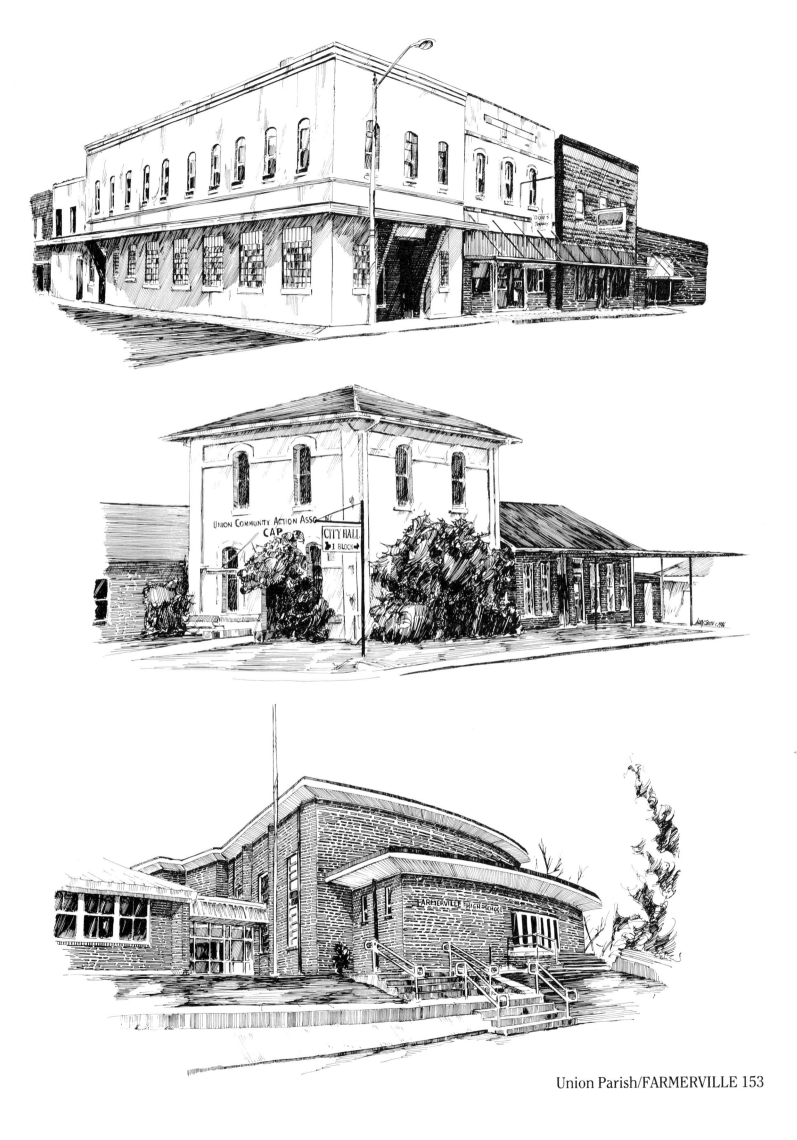

Jena

Through the trees of the Great Pine Forest known as the Choctaw District, rode the preacher Nolly. It was early in the 1800s, on a return trip from preaching the gospel and patriotism to a band of soldiers, that his horse bolted and he froze to death in the flooded Hemphill Creek.

This beautiful running creek and the fertile lands it flowed through were purchased by the Hemphills. It was not until fifty years later that the Hemp's Creek Settlement really began to develop. People from miles around came to the Baker mill which was equipped to make corn meal and gin cotton, especially on Saturday when the corn meal was made. Soon a store was opened on the Harrisonburg-Alexandria road to sell to the settlers of the area. The next year another store opened on the other side of the Road. Hemp's Creek was growing.

When the post office decided to discard all Creeks and Bayous from the names of its post offices, a new name was needed. A contest was held and names were entered. A resident's brother, who was visiting, entered the name of his hometown in Illinois. It won and Hemp's Creek became Jena, the eventual parish seat of Catahoula.

Louisiana Proud

IT WAS MURDER!

Murder in the dead of night on the Steamer St. Mary, and it did not end the bitter Jones-Liddell feud that had lasted almost 20 years. Friends of the slain General Liddell ended this saga of bloody vengeance at the small hotel where Colonel Jones and his two sons were being held by the sheriff. The Colonel and one of his sons were killed while the other escaped. This feud took the lives of at least five of Catahoula's most prominent citizens, and ended the influence of two of the most cultured and outstanding families in this part of the State.

A year later the town was platted and laid out in lots by the widow Jones, who owned the entire tract of land. This Spanish grant of 1,000 acres was named Jonesville in her honor. It is situated in the angle between Little and Black Rivers, and is in the heart of a rich agricultural district. Due to its location, Jonesville grew and developed rapidly at the expense of her older sister city, Trinity, which was across the river.

In the middle of the town there was an Indian Mound, which was verified by the Smithsonian Institute as the second largest ever discovered in the U.S. It has been removed and the dirt used for the building of the existing bridge spanning the Black River. Yearly floods prevented the town from developing as fast at it could have, but the coming of the railroad and the building of a ring levee changed this.

Louisiana Proud

Jonesville

The early settlers floated toward unknown destinations in small crude crafts. They relied on homemade paddles and oars to direct their descent. The Mississippi, with its changing currents, sand bars and floating debris, was very dangerous. But compared to what was around the bend, they seemed like nothing at all.

They had already been spotted by the lookouts in the trees. The word had been spread and the ambush made ready. As their crafts made the turn in the river, the pirates of Captain Bunch descended upon them. This turn in the river became known as Bunch's Bend. To reach the small settlement below the Bend, with life and cargo intact, seemed surely an act of Providence. And so it was named.

Lake Providence

Louisiana Proud

The early 1800s witnessed an earthquake which destroyed the strong hold of the Bunch Gang, and cut a new canal, leaving a six mile long ox-bow lake. With the increased stream of settlers and safer river travel, the small settlement became the Town of Providence. When the Parish of Carroll was formed, the Town of Providence became the logical choice for the parish seat. It remained so for twenty years, until the population had filtered into the interior. Tangled brush, dense cane thickets and other natural obstructions created hazards for the people west of Bayou Macon when governmental proceedings were necessary. The seat of justice was moved to Floyd. The problem was still the same, only this time the people of Providence complained. The issue was settled when the Parish was divided, along the Bayou, into East and West Carroll Parishes.

The Town of Providence settled into an agricultural life style. The rich fertile lands around the lake and the yearly Mississippi overflows replenished the top soil, providing a great life style for a few and a comfortable one for the rest. Cotton was king and thousand acre plantations were common.

Major fighting during the War took place here, with at first, the Confederates, aided by Quantrelle's Guerrillas, taking the victories. Reinforcements soon gave the Federals the advantage, and it was here that Grant gave the order to dig a canal from the town to the river in order to capture Vicksburg. The Post Office, confusing the Town of Providence with Providence, Rhode Island, requested the name be changed. The present town of Lake Providence is the second location, the first was located farther north and is now a part of the Mississippi.

As the War ended, Lake Providence returned to its agricultural life style and more peaceful ways.

Monroe

It took almost one hundred years to develop the interior of Louisiana. Settling first on the main river routes, the rich Delta area was left to the Indians and a few hardy trappers. Finally Spanish governor Miro commissioned Don Juan Filhoil to establish a post on the Ouachita River. He traveled as far north as Arkansas, but had seen a better spot lower on the river. Returning there, he built a fort and waited for the settlers. Here the Post of the Ouachita, later called Fort Miro, safeguarded the territory and became a central spot for the traders to meet and ship their goods.

It was left to the Marquis de Maison Rouge and the Baron de Bastrop to develop the land. They were both granted large areas of land with the stipulation that they bring in permanent settlers. The stipulation that no American families were to be allowed to settle hindered the growth of the area. Large plantations soon developed and cotton became their major product.

One day, preceded by a toot and whistle, the first steamboat pulled up at the docks. Everyone came to see the strange sight and soon much excitement and gaiety was evident. After a party on the boat, given by the captain, the prominent townsfolk decided to change the name of their town. The boat and the president were both named James Monroe, and in honor of them, along with the realization of the new era that was just starting, they called their town Monroe.

With transportation open for a least seventy-five miles in any direction, Monroe very rapidly became the town of north central Louisiana. Merchants and Middlemen prospered. The population did not grow as one would expect, largely due to the large plantations of the time, but its influence was felt throughout the state and especially in the northern section.

Monroe was basically a rough frontier town until the railroads opened the area for easier access. It survived the War with only a few small skirmishes and after the dark days of Reconstruction slowly continued to grow.

Louisiana Proud

Oak Grove

Through the early evening dusk the lone storekeeper could make out two figures emerging silently from the wooded background. They were Yankee soldiers. The came to a halt in front of his store and waited for him to come out.

"What do you have for sale?", they demanded.

"Pins and Hooks, Pins and Hooks!", he replied.

They rode back into the woods and the trading post came to be known as the Pin Hook Store. Soon the area and the new settlement around the store came to be known as Pin Hook.

After the War ended, the country started getting on with the business of living. Strangers were arriving all the time. There were others who were not so strange to this environment. Seen at parties or on dark nights as silent figures poling down the bayou to visit friends, they were welcomed. The curly haired young man with the limp and courteous manner, who could tell a story with the best of them, was Frank James. Frank and his brother, Jessie, along with their kind, were looked upon with favor, as they did much to keep the area peaceful. Few of the bands of Yankee Raiders were bold enough to pillage this area.

As the population shifted, so did the parish seat. Originally located in Floyd, which was by-passed by the railroad and left to die, the government moved to Pin Hook. When the post office moved it took the name Oak Grove. The ringing of the bell signalled that court was in session. This old bell, which had once resided in the old courthouse at Floyd, had also been rung as a beacon for people who were lost in the surrounding swamps. Even before the railroad came, a walk down main street would take you by the Andrew Jackson General Merchandise Store, the Bank of Oak Grove, Dr. Bliss's Drug Store or any of a half dozen other prominent Oak Grove establishments.

In the extreme eastern portion of the vast Ouachita Parish was a small settlement.

Here on the east side of the Beouf River, a store was established and several settlers were attracted to the rich land. They called their settlement Little Creek. When the two railroads crossed here, new impetus was added to the growth of the area. The man who ran that first store was James Ray, and he had a brother in Monroe. His brother, John, had large land holdings in this and other sections. John was also a politician, in fact, he was the Republican leader from Ouachita during Reconstruction. Using his influence, he introduced a bill which created a new parish. It was called Richland because of the promise of the soil. The settlement at the junction became the parish seat. It was instantly named Rayville.

The first courthouse meeting was held the same year in a wooden plank building. Three years later, as the population increased, a new courthouse was built. The 1890s saw two fires which destroyed much of the town. Rebuilding was almost instantaneous and the town of Rayville was quickly rebuilt into one of the prettiest towns of the northeast.

Rayville

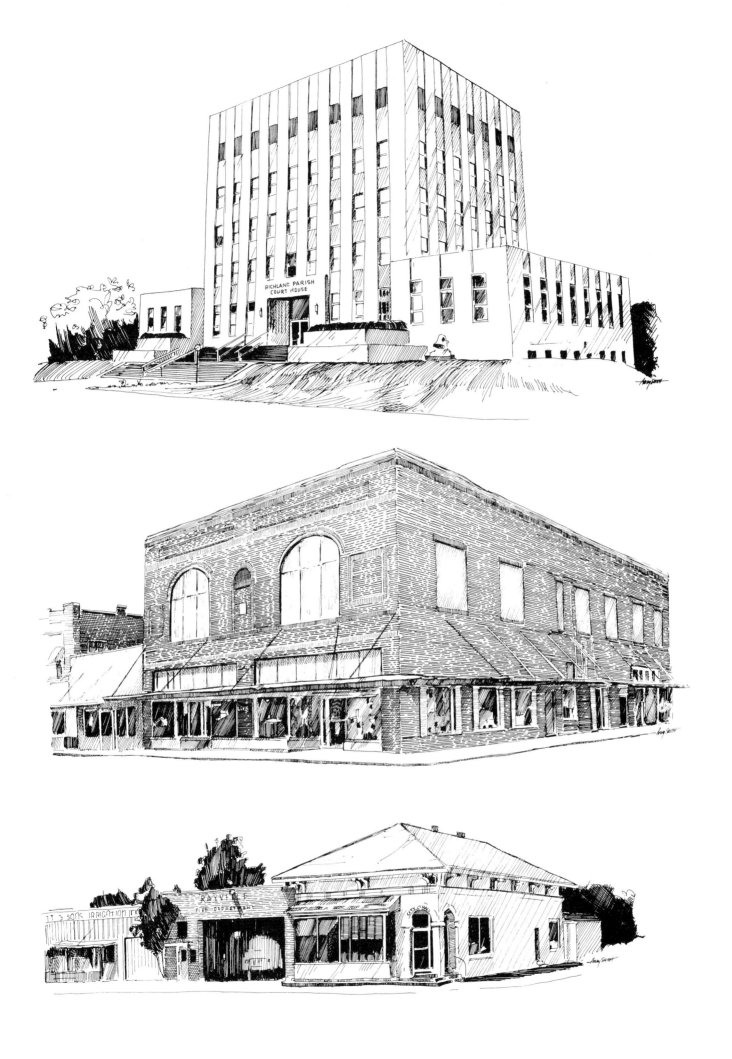

Pleasant View was the name of the plantation sitting on the bank of the Mississippi and the home of the Bondurant's. He, a captain in the Tensas Rifles, away at the front with his company; she, a graceful lady left home to care for the plantation.

As news of Grant's March through Louisiana came closer, it was anything but a pleasant sight as Mrs. Bondurant ordered her slaves to move the 100 bales of ready-to-market cotton to the banks of the river. Dousing them with kerosene, she ordered them set afire, then left for Texas. Grant's anger was showered on the main house in the form of musket and cannon ball, the marks of which can still be seen today.

It was not to a violent area that John Densmore first came. He built a cabin, a store and ran a ferry across the river to the commercial center at Rodney, Mississippi. His site became known as Densmore Landing and developed into a shipping area for the many plantations in the area. Once on a part of the main channel of the river, the town took the name of St. Joseph for the ox-bow lake of the same name. Being a child of the plantation system, St. Joseph grew slowly until the coming of the railroad opened new markets. St. Joseph remains the largest town and the seat of government in Tensas Parish.

St. Joseph

Louisiana Proud

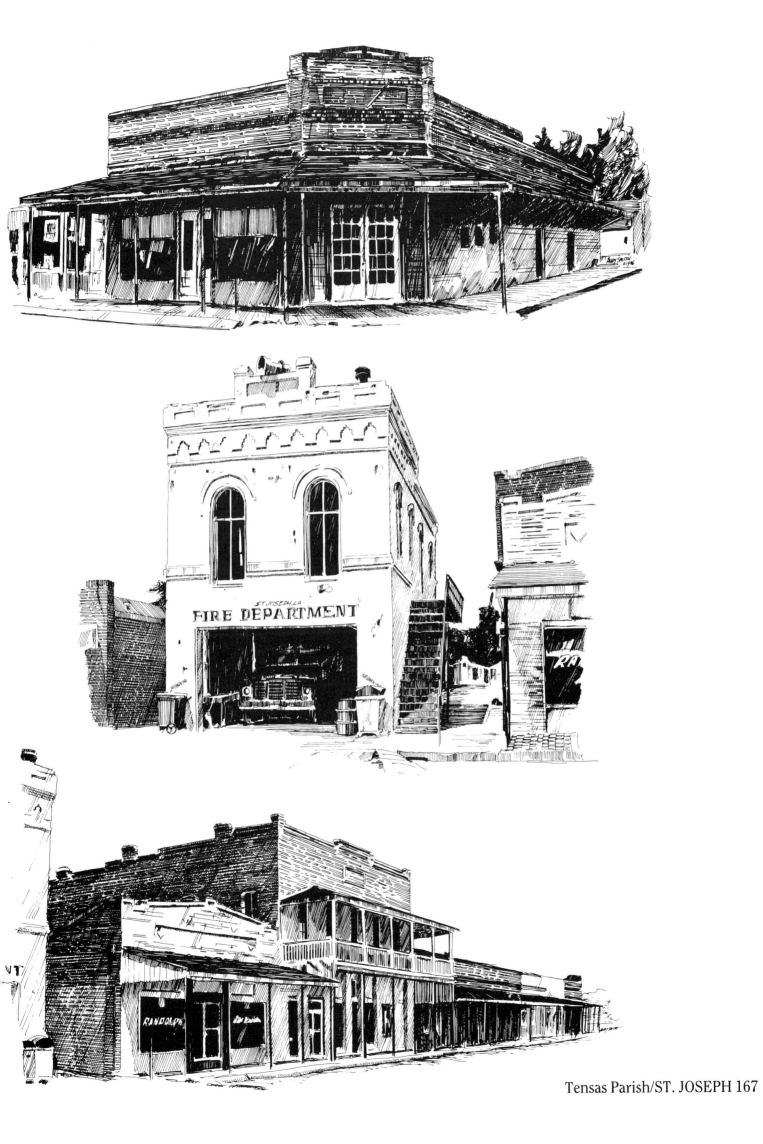

Tallulah

In the 1850s, Richmond was the parish seat of Madison Parish and the natural selection for the train route. Important reasons indeed, but not as important as the lady to the north whose charms enchanted the railroad engineer. It was he who routed the Vicksburg, Shreveport and Mississippi tracks through her land. And, it was he, who after the tracks were laid, suffered when she switched her affections to another. The widow got her railroad and the engineer the right to name the town. In honor of an old sweetheart in Georgia, and to spite the widow, he named it Tallulah.

Tallulah was a cotton town, located on the banks of the Round-Away Bayou which snaked its way through the townsite. Sitting in the River Basin Swamp, Tallulah often was victimized by water and mud during overflows and floods. Each time she rebuilt and began anew on freshly deposited top soil. These lands attracted many farmers and soon stately mansions dotted the bayou. It was in one of these, the Adams House, that the parish records were hidden as Grant's army descended upon Richmond, the seat of government. Richmond, was destroyed and the town of Delta, seizing upon the opportunity, built a courthouse and became the new parish seat. Since Tallulah was larger, feelings were high in favor of moving the seat there. The people of Delta refused. And it was not until a dark moonless night in 1883 that a group of horsemen rode into Delta and, under the camouflage of darkness, stole the parish records and seals.

The next morning, upon discovering the nights proceedings, the people of Delta became outraged. They came to Tallulah demanding the return of the Documents. When the answer was "No," they returned to an empty courthouse.

Tallulah has remained the parish seat ever since.

Madison Parish/TALLULAH 169

Vidalia

Don Jose Vidal, realizing that the United States was going to force the Spanish to vacate Natchez, petitioned the King of Spain for lands in Spanish territory. He was given the land across the river from the Plaza de Natchez, and thus became Commandant of Fort Panmure. It was the oldest post in Louisiana on the Mississippi above New Orleans. One of his first acts was to change the name to Fort Concord.

Out of this land of river bullies, bandits and gamblers, and on the edge of an undeveloped great wilderness, Vidal had the town laid out. He donated the land for public buildings and for the first school in the parish. He built the first steam sawmill in addition to a cotton gin and a blacksmith shop. Soon a branch of the Mechanics and Traders Bank was opened. Businesses and people came and settled, and a town developed under the watchful and protective eye of the Commandant of the Poste de Concordia.

It was here that the "Sand Bar" fight helped Jim Bowie and his long knife add to their fame.

With the Louisiana Purchase completed, the Commandant Americanized his name to Joseph Vidal. In honor of the fort, the parish took its name, Concordia; in honor of the man, the town was called Vidalia.

Louisiana Proud

Winnsboro

The entire area which is now Franklin Parish was once a sea of thick bamboo like cane. Towering over this shimmering scene were gum, huge oak and giant cypress trees, which lined the streams and bayous. So impenetrable was this interior wilderness that settlement of the parish took place only along the navigable streams of the Beouf River on the western edge, and Bayou Macon on the eastern side.

A large Indian civilization on the Beouf Prairie left its mark on the land in the form of giant mounds. In some mysterious way the Indians had disappeared and left only these mounds to be remembered by. The danger to the early pioneer was the Indians who were presently occupying the territory. They, too, chose the lands along the streams and rivers and fought to keep them. Many settlers were killed during this time of early colonization. After 1800, the French Army chased the Indians to Lake Lewis and completely defeated the tribe, ending their era. From then on, they would no longer hinder the advancement of settlement.

By the 1850s enough hardy families had settled, and, as they had grown tired of going to Harrisonburg for legal matters, suggested a new parish be created. John Winn, a pioneer and land owner, introduced the bill to create Franklin Parish. A disagreement over where the courthouse should be located developed. It was decided when John Willis donated 160 acres of land almost in the center of the parish. The parish seat was thus established and called Winnsboro in honor of Senator Winn.

ACKNOWLEDGEMENTS

For the past five years this project has needed the help of others. I would like to thank them also.

Al, Mike, Sara, Evelyn and all the others at Baton Rouge Printing who went out of their way to help me with the printing of the posters calendars, brochures and all the collateral material I needed.

Bobby L. Freeman, Lt. Governor wrote the foreward.

Tom Clark kept the computer running and set up the programs that were needed.

Eileen R. Sonnier and Dennis A. DeShon helped in editing, proofreading, and punctuation.

George Nance set the type.

Ed Reed lent his political and literary advice.

SOURCES

Survey of Union Parish Louisiana, Resources and Facilities; Vermilion Parish, Resources and Facilities; Louisiana Places; Mr. Kentzel's Covington; Red River Parish, Resources and Facilities; Richland Parish, Resources and Facilities; Lafayette Parish, Resources and Facilities; Lincoln Parish, Resources and Facilities; The History of Sabine Parish; Tall Pines, The Story of Vernon Parish; Desoto Parish, Resources and Facilities; Evangeline Parish, Economic Redevelopment Commission Inc.; East Carroll Parish, Resources and Facilities; A Village So Small (The Town of Oak Ridge); Tangipahoa Crossings, Excursions Into Tangipahoa History; Lecompte, Plantation Town In Transition; Our Pride . . . Pointe Coupee; Calcasieu Parish, Resources and Facilities, 1945; Catahoula Parish, Resources and Facilities, 1948; Claiborne Parish, Resources and Facilities, 1948; A Brief History of Vernon Parish, Louisiana, by John T. Cupit; History of Avoyelles Parish Louisiana, by Corinne L. Saucier, M.A.; Cheneyville Yesterday, 1812-1980; Louisiana Municipal Ass'n. Lovely Louisiana, 1961; A History of St. Mary Parish, by Bernard Broussard; Southwest Louisiana Biographical and Historical by William Henry Perrin; East Feliciana, Louisiana Past and Present, Sketches of the Pioneers by H. Skipwith, Written in 1892; Mississippi Louisiana, Border Country, Logan; Plantation Life in the Florida Parishes of Louisiana, 1836-1846, Barrow; Between the Rivers, A West Carroll Chronicle by Florence Stewart McKoin; Cabanocey by Lillain C. Bourgeois, (St. James Parish); Once Upon a River, A History of Pineville, Louisiana by Elaine H. Brister; Caddo:1000, A History of the Shreveport Area, by Viola Carruth; The Red River: A Historical Perspective, produced by Commercial National Bank of Shreveport, La.; New Iberia; Essays on the Town and People., compiled by Glenn R. Conrad; The Center: A History of the Development of Lafayette, Louisiana, by J. Philip Dismukes; Jackson Parish Louisiana: published by Jackson Parish Chamber of Commerce, Jonesboro, La.; A Place to Remember, East Carroll Parish, La. by Georgia Payne Durham Pinkston; Morehouse Parish, Louisiana, Resources and Facilities; Louisiana's Historic Towns by Jess DeHart; Eastern Louisiana, A History, by Fredrick William Williamson; The Town That Crayfish Built, A History of Henderson, Louisiana by Marjorie R. Esman, PH.D.; The Attakapas Country, A History of Lafayette Parish, Louisiana by Harry Lewis Grifin; Baker: The First 200 years, 1776-1976; The Lafourche Country: The People and the Land, edited by Philip D. Uzee; Chronicles of West Baton Rouge by Elizabeth Kellough and Leona Mayeux; A Narrative History of Breaux Bridge, Once Called "La Pointe"; Livingston Parish, Resources and Facilities; The Story of the West Florida Rebellion, by Stanley Clisby Arthur; Historic Jefferson Parish, From Shore to Shore by Betsy Swanson; The Free State, A History and Place-Names Study of Livingston Parish; Lincoln Parish History, Lincoln Parish Bicentennial Committee; Historical and Pictorial Review of the past 75 years of the City of Ruston; La Salle Parish, Resources and Facilities; Fullerton, The Mill, The Town, The People, 1907-1927 by Anna C. Burns; St. Bernard Parish, Resources and Facilities; Jefferson Davis Parish, Resources and Facilities; Washington Parish, Resources and Facilities; Story of Ascension Parish, Sidney A. Marchand 1931; Grant Parish, Louisiana; Grant Parish, Louisiana; A History, by Harrison and McNeely; Saint John The Baptist Parish on the Corridor of History; The Opelousas Country-with a History of Evangeline Parish by Robert Cahn; Natchitoches, Oldest Settlement in the Louisiana Purchase, by Association of Natchitoches Women; Pointe Coupee Parish, Resources and Facilities; Iberville Parish, Resources and Facilities; Iberville Parish History by Judy Riffel; Acadia Parish, Resources and Facilities; Acadia Parish, Louisiana, A History to 1900, by Mary Alice Fontenot; St. Tammany Parish, by Frederick S. Ellis; St. Tammany Parish, Resources and Facilities; Tensas Parish, Resources and Facilities; Claiborne Parish, Resources and Facilities; The History of Claiborne Parish, Louisiana, by Harris and Hulse; Louisiana Today, 1924 – Louisiana Department of Agriculture and Immigration; Do You Know Louisiana, Louisiana Department of Commerce and Industry; Historic Claiborne by Claiborne Parish Historical Association; Webster Parish, Resources and Facilities; Union Parish, Resources and Facilities; Louisiana by Fortier-Vol. 1; Louisiana by Fortier-Vol. 2; Avoyelles Parish, Resources and Facilities; Beauregard Parish, Resources and Facilities; Avoyelles: Crossroads of Louisiana by Louisiana Commission des Avoyelle; Sabine Parish History – Land of Green Gold, by Amos Lee Armstrong; Ouachita Parish, Resources and Facilities; Louisiana, A Guide to the State – Writers Program; Madison Parish, Resources and Facilities; Reprint of the Rapides Parish Section of Biographical and Historical Memoirs of Northwest Louisiana with Newly Compiled Name Index-Index compiled by Benjamin E. Achee; Caldwell Parish in Slices by H. Ted Woods; I Dug Up Houma, Terrebonne by Helen Emmeline Wurslow; Rapides Parish History by Sue Eakin; As I Remember by Hildebrand (Jefferson Davis Parish); Historic Cotile by Barber; A Essay on Lower Louisiana by Stephen Duplantier; Webster Parish Centennial, 1871-1971; Rapides Parish, Louisiana, A History by G.P. Whittington; Northeast Louisiana by Williamson; History of St. Martin Parish, Louisiana Volume 1; History of St. Charles Parish to 1973 by Henry E. Yoes III; A Town Named Elton by Joanne Foley Putnam; East Feliciana Parish 1824-1974, "Land of Seven Springs and Seven Pastures" by Boatner; Concordia Parish, Resources and Facilities; Nostalgic Notes on St. James Parish, Then and Now by Marie Pilkington Campell; Biographical and Historical Memoirs of Northwest Louisiana; Franklin Parish, Resources and Facilities; Records and Recollections of Thibodaux, La. by William Littlejohn Martin; Winn Parish Louisiana 1852-1985; Plaquemines Parish, by J.B. Meyer; The Land of Promise, by J.B. Meyer; Old New Orleans by Stanley Clisby Arthur; The New Orleans Vignette – 1979; The Settlement of the German Coast of Louisiana and the Creoles of German Descent by John Hanno Deiler; St. Charles Parish, Resources and Facilities; The New Louisiana by John Klorer; Zachary, Faces and Places.